Getting Started in
Debate

Lynn Goodnight

NATIONAL TEXTBOOK COMPANY • Lincolnwood, Illinois

CONTENTS

ACKNOWLEDGMENTS

There are a number of people without whom this book could not have been completed. My editor, Judith Clayton, has been invaluable on this project. She has been patient, supportive, challenging, and a good listener. Without my husband, Tom Goodnight, I could not have finished this book. He read and reread each of the chapters and provided valued suggestions. He was also there with support whenever I seemed to need it. A special thanks to Mrs. Judy Dorsett, my eighth grade speech teacher. She introduced me to the world of debate. And to my parents who served as chaperons on many debate trips and supported me in my love for debate.

The publishers and author would like to thank the following people for their valuable assistance in the development of this book: Odis Richardson, Du Sable High School; Alexandra Hoecherl, Appleton High School; and Drusilla Murray, Hyde Park High School.

Getting Started in Debate is designed for the student with no background in debate. It is based on the philosophy that debate teaches skills applicable to all walks of life. Debate helps develop critical thinking, courage, organization, and leadership and investigative skills. This text helps the beginning debater to know how to think through an idea and develop arguments for or against it, and how to anticipate arguments someone else might make.

The research skills students develop through debate can be very useful. Debate provides hands-on experience in learning about the various sources of research. *Getting Started in Debate* provides a step-by-step guide on how to use library indexes to aid one's research. Information on how to find and use government documents is included. It is easier to argue for change if one knows how and why the current laws were put into place.

Getting Started in Debate uses a developmental approach, heavily supported by activities. The work/text format is designed to involve students in activities while learning about debate. "Questions for Discussion" helps students become familiar with key terms and concepts. The "Activities" are designed to help beginning debaters work toward an actual debate. By the end of Chapter Eight, students should have a basic understanding of the rules of debate and enough evidence and ideas on a specific topic to actually debate.

Chapter One introduces the student to a definition of debate. A number of lifeskills students develop through debate such as analysis, critical thinking and listening, open-mindedness, and teamwork are discussed.

Chapter Two defines the five basic elements of debate. The problem area, proposition, affirmative, and negative are explained. The fifth element, flow sheeting, is described, and a sample flow of a debate is included.

Chapter Three outlines the different debate formats and speaker responsibilities. Standard debate, Cross-examination debate, and Lincoln-Douglas debate are described with their time limits. Eight debate speeches are outlined along with the responsibilities of the speaker during a given speech.

Chapter Four takes a look at the types of propositions. Students will learn to distinguish between a proposition of fact, value, or policy.

Chapter Five discusses research skills. Basic questions on what to research, where to look, how to decide what evidence is good, and what to do with the evidence once it's found are addressed here.

Chapter Six takes the student to the library. The student learns about the sources available in a library and how to find them. A number of special indexes that can open the door to specialized literature are described here.

Chapter Seven introduces the affirmative position. Students will learn what the affirmative must do to prove that a change should be made. Two case formats, and how they can be used to present the affirmative idea, are described.

Chapter Eight presents the negative position. The ways of defending against arguments are described. The rules governing the negative are outlined. The concept of disadvantages is explained.

A *Teacher's Manual* to accompany the text is available. Included in the *Manual* are the answers to "Questions for Discussion" and "Activities," background for teaching each chapter, a series of lesson plans for 9-18 weeks, a sample debate ballot, and test questions.

1

An Introduction

When the word *debate* comes up in a conversation, most people think of the Presidential Debates. Beginning with the Kennedy-Nixon Debate in 1960, political debates have been the arena in which candidates can "confront" each other and deal with issues directly. As you will learn in this book, the format used for political debates does not set the stage for a true confrontation between candidates. Most political debates are, at best, modified press conference forums in which questions and issues are chosen by a panel rather than the candidates. In this text we will look at debate in the academic setting. It will help you to gain an understanding of the nature of true debate and to develop valuable lifeskills. After reading this book, some of you may decide to participate in academic debate. After reading this chapter you should understand the following debate terms:

affirmative	negative
debate	present system
evidence	proof
judge	proposition
logical reasoning	

DEBATE—A DEFINITION

Debate is defined as a regulated discussion of a proposition by two matched sides. It provides reasoned arguments for and against a given *proposition.* The proposition is a statement that is open to interpretation. It is a statement about which reasonable people may accept arguments on either side. Debate may also be used by an individual to reach a decision. For example, a student may debate in his or her own mind whether to take a course in home economics or one in automobile repair. The student hopes to make a decision based on good reasoning and evidence.

In a court of law the defense and the prosecution debate the guilt or innocence of the accused before a jury. They do this by presenting evidence through witnesses and refuting the evidence through cross-examination. In our legislative branch of government, bills are presented to the House and Senate and then debated. In the history of the Senate, debating skills have helped shape history. Senators Henry Clay, Daniel Webster, John C. Calhoun, Robert M. LaFollette, and Robert A. Taft used their debating skills to provide leadership and to help clarify issues of great importance to this nation. In 1957 the Senate designated these men as Senate Immortals due largely to their abilities as debaters. But what is academic debate?

An academic debate is approximately one hour in length. The actual length may vary depending on the specific format used. (Debate formats are covered in Chapter 3.) In each academic debate, there are two teams. Each team has two members. The *affirmative* team argues that a change should be made in the present system. The present system is the current state of affairs: the laws, regulations, and rules that we live by. The *negative* team defends the present system. It argues that although the present system might have a few minor problems, they are problems that can be solved without a major change (a new law, regulation, or rule).

How It Works   Suppose, for example, that the topic for debate is the student dress code. The proposition might be worded this way:

Resolved: That appropriate dress for school should be left up to the individual student.

The affirmative team would want to show how the current dress code (the present system) restricts student freedom in choosing what to wear to school. The affirmative would try to prove this claim by documenting the school's dress code rules. Next, the affirmative would show how these rules prevent students from wearing what they want to school. Then, the affirmative would propose the elimination of all rules relating to student dress. The affirmative would also show that the elimination of a student dress code would not be harmful. If there are any advantages to eliminating the dress code, the affirmative would want to outline these, as well.

The negative's job would be to defend the present system (the current dress code). The negative would argue that there is nothing wrong with the present dress code. The negative might show that the dress code is very liberal and that most students presently wear what they want and do not violate school rules. The negative might also argue that the students participate in making the rules that comprise the dress code. The negative would also want to discuss the disadvantages of eliminating the dress code. A disadvantage might be that not all students want to follow the latest fad in fashion. Some students cannot afford to buy new clothes as each fad comes along. A student dress code gives these students a reason not to give in to peer pressure to dress in the latest fad. To eliminate the dress code would be to take away an important "crutch." Many teenagers need such "crutches" to help them through their adolescent years as they learn that it is OK to say no.

In order for either team to convince someone that they are right, the arguments for or against the student dress code must be proven. This proof can be logical reasoning, evidence, or a combination of the two. To use logical reasoning means to explain why a particular argument makes sense. Sometimes an argument can be explained to the satisfaction of everyone in a debate through common sense or with facts that are assumed to be true by most people. The preferred form of proof is *evidence*. Evidence is the information used to form the basis of an argument. When you are looking for evidence to prove an argument, you are looking for someone, respected by others, to support the argument you are making. Such statements are usually found in books, newsletters, newspapers, magazines, news releases, journals, and interviews. For example, if the negative wants to prove that student dress codes are essential and valuable, they must provide evidence. They would want to research educational journals for articles (written by teachers and administrators) that discuss student dress codes. Popular magazines aimed at teenage audiences may also have articles on dress codes. Newspapers may also have information if there has been some controversy in a school involving students and the dress code. The school newspaper should not be overlooked. How to find sources, identify pieces of evidence, and put them in a usable form is discussed in detail in Chapter 5.

QUESTIONS FOR DISCUSSION

1. What is a *debate*?

2. The team supporting the proposition is called the _____.

3. The team refuting, or arguing against, the proposition is called the _____.

4. In debate why does the affirmative or negative need proof to support their arguments?

5. There are two types of proof. Identify each and explain the advantages and/or disadvantages of each.

JUDGING

Each debate is evaluated by a *judge*. The judge is usually a single person or a panel of three people who evaluate a debate against certain ideal standards of debating and decide who wins and who loses. Criteria include analysis, reasoning, evidence, organization, refutation, and delivery. The audience or class listening to a debate may serve as the judge. In the classroom, students might be asked to vote for the side that did the better job of debating, or "won," the debate. In presidential and other political debates in this country, the voter or the American public in general is the judge. After political debates, polls are taken to determine who "won" the debate. The media usually evaluate political debates and decide "who did the better job of debating." This often influences the judgment of the audience at large.

TIMEKEEPING

To keep track of each debater's speaking time, a timekeeper is used. It is the job of the timekeeper to let the speaker know how much speaking or preparation time has elapsed. The timekeeper does this with time cards. The time is counted down in minute increments (8, 7, 6, 5, etc.) until the last minute, when 30-second increments are used (1, 30 seconds, stop). When all of the allotted time has been used, the speaker is allowed to finish the last sentence and then must stop. When a timekeeper is not available, time can be kept in one of two ways. First, the judge can keep time. Second, each team can keep time for itself. The latter should be done only when no other option is available. Rules governing individual speech time limits, preparation time, and speaker responsibilities are covered in more detail in Chapter 3.

WHY DEVELOP DEBATE SKILLS?

Debate is more than an academic activity. It develops skills and values that will prove important to every participant. You do not need to become a lawyer, politician, or speech major to benefit from debate. Admittedly, not all the skills and values are unique to debate. However, debate is an invaluable way to practice these skills and acquire these values. For some people, debate may be the only opportunity to be exposed to these skills and values.

Debate Offers Preparation for Leadership

A good leader is able to state a goal, make a plan, and then work to achieve that goal. This may require convincing others to participate and proving to people in positions of authority that the goal is worth achieving. There are few classes and activities in our schools that teach this ability. Our society is in great need of articulate men and women who can analyze a problem, win the agreement of others under stress, and persuade others to take the steps necessary to put the plan into action. Students who fulfill these qualifications often rise to positions of leadership in their business, professional, or civic undertakings after high school or college.

Many people who have achieved leadership positions were debaters while they were in school and they regard that experience as a significant factor in the attainment of their positions. A survey of 160 senators, congressmen and women, governors, Supreme Court justices, Cabinet members, and other leaders revealed that 100 of the leaders had high school or college debate experience. All of the 100 found their debate experience helpful in their careers, and 90 classified the experience as "greatly helpful" or "invaluable." Of the 60 who did not have debate experience, 26 expressed regret that they did not have it in high school or college.

QUESTION FOR DISCUSSION

1. In debate, what helps to develop one's leadership capabilities?

ACTIVITY

1. In light of your current plans for the future, explain how debate will help you develop leadership capability.

Debate Provides for Investigation and Intensive Analysis of Contemporary Problems

The general public often has only a superficial knowledge of significant contemporary problems. Because debate resolutions often deal with such problems, debate participation provides the opportunity to investigate and analyze these problems. Thus, debaters can acquire a better than average knowledge of current problems, as well as the skills to analyze critically the problems they will encounter in the future.

Debate Develops the Ability to Make Prompt Analytical Responses

Today's world moves at a very rapid pace. Often, there is no time or opportunity to respond adequately to an issue or challenge. In today's world of instant communication, a lawyer, business executive, or private citizen may be in a position that requires a prompt, analytical response. Debate teaches the individual to do this. In the course of one hour, arguments are made and responded to. The speeches are prepared during other debaters' speeches or in the brief time allowed between speeches.

QUESTIONS FOR DISCUSSION

1. How can debate help you to develop an analytical mind?

2. Why is it valuable to develop your analytical capabilities?

Debate Develops Critical Listening

People tend to tune out much of what is said around them and directly to them. For this reason, many businesses send their employees to classes where they learn listening skills. In a debate if you daydream while an opponent speaks, your reply is likely to be ineffective and irrelevant. Thus, debaters learn to listen attentively to their opponents and to record their arguments precisely on the flow sheet (the form used for taking notes; see Chapter 2). In this way, they are able to tailor their responses to the point— sometimes even using the words their opponents have used—and to turn their opponents' arguments to their own advantage. The ability to listen critically is widely recognized as an important skill.

ACTIVITIES

1. Attend the next PTA, school board, or city council meeting and identify instances in which speakers are not listening to what is being said. What difference did this make in the proceedings? How might arguments later made by the listener have been changed had he or she been listening more critically?

2. At the same meeting identify instances in which the audience made arguments or statements that were flawed because they had not listened attentively during the proceedings.

Debate Develops Courage

Debate helps students to develop courage by requiring them to research and formulate a case and then defend that case against strong opposition. Skillful opponents will have no trouble finding flaws in an argument you thought flawless. It would be easy for you to panic, make a retreat, and avoid the problem. As a debater, however, you can't just give up. The situation requires that you defend your position. Debaters learn to discipline themselves, concentrate on the problem, organize their thoughts, and respond to arguments effectively. With time and practice most debaters realize that they can think on their feet and defend a position. They also realize that most of their opponents are not invincible or unbeatable. This process helps students to develop self-confidence and to acquire the ability to function under stress.

Debate Encourages Effective Speech Composition and Delivery

Since composition and delivery of the debate speech are among the factors that determine the effectiveness of arguments, debaters are encouraged to select, arrange, and present their materials in accordance with the best principles of public speaking. Debating places a premium on extemporaneous delivery, requiring speakers to think on their feet. Typically, debaters will speak before many different audiences: a single judge, a panel of judges, a class, a group of people at a meeting and sometimes even a radio or TV audience. Each of these situations provides new challenges for students. Constant adaptation to the judge, the audience, and to the speech situation develops flexibility and facility in thinking and speaking.

Debate Teaches Organization

The debater learns to place arguments in a framework that makes the ideas easy to follow and hard to forget. In debate, the judge and the other team take nothing for granted. If organization is poor and the argument is difficult to understand, the judge will be confused, and the other team will exploit its advantage. When a speech is unorganized and confusing, it is unlikely that anyone will find the arguments convincing. The need to be clear and convincing in debate forces debaters to become highly skilled in organizing their presentations. This skill can also help the student in writing term papers, studying for exams, arguing for changes in school policy, and developing personally and professionally.

QUESTIONS FOR DISCUSSION

1. Why is the *delivery* of a speech important in persuading an audience?

2. What impact does a poorly organized speech have on an audience?

ACTIVITIES

1. Attend a meeting of a student organization, the school board, or the city council. Identify a speech that was poorly written or delivered and explain what was wrong with it and how it affected the audience.

2. Identify a speech that was poorly or well organized. Outline the strong or weak points of the organization. What could have been done differently for a more effective and persuasive appeal?

Debate Teaches Critical Thinking

Debaters need to know why they are using a particular type of approach, method of organization, or presentation style. They must seek the best evidence—from the library, from correspondence, or from other resources discussed later in Chapter 6. They must think about the evidence being used and understand exactly what it does for their arguments. They must think about the consequences of each argument and evaluate its worth. What are the demands of the topic for debate? What are the potential strengths and weaknesses of the research materials that have been gathered? Which approach to analysis, based on the evidence seems strongest in the debate? What might the opponents be expected to do? How might the judges be expected to react to the opposition's arguments? The critical thinking that develops in the course of answering such questions is a skill that will prove invaluable in life.

Debate Teaches Open-Mindedness

When we are trying to develop an argument, it is difficult to remain open-minded on the issues. Often, our personal biases create a blind spot, and we are unable to see the reasons behind someone else's position. As a result, we may not be able to anticipate what others will say against our position. In debate, however, we are forced to consider what the opposition might say. What are the reasons for the opposition's position? What is the evidence to support that position? What is the quality of that evidence? Does the reasoning make sense? We use the answers to these questions to help establish and support our own position. And we learn that on almost any issue, we can find good reasons for supporting either side.

QUESTIONS FOR DISCUSSION

1. Why is critical thinking important? What advantage does the critical thinker have over others who have not developed this skill?

2. What are the possible consequences of approaching an argument without an open mind?

3. How does having an open mind on an issue help you in preparing your position?

ACTIVITIES

1. Using an issue of importance in the news, outline the pros and cons on the issue. Then, identify which side of the issue you personally favor. Are there more reasons on the side you favor? If so, try to equalize the pros and cons.

2. Collect five articles or newspaper clippings on the issue chosen in Activity 1. Determine if each article was written with an open mind. Identify any biases you see in the articles. Would these articles be good for either research material or for evidence for or against the issue? Why or why not?

Debate Enhances Cooperation and Teamwork

To begin with, debate requires teamwork. The two members on each team must work together. The affirmative team members must research and understand the arguments comprising their case. A negative team that does not work together runs the risk of contradicting itself. The first negative speaker might argue that the problem the affirmative has outlined does not exist or is unimportant. The second negative speaker could then argue that it would be harmful to correct the problem outlined by the affirmative. These two arguments contradict each other. Both cannot be true at the same time. There may be evidence proving both arguments but the negative would not want to use both of those arguments in the same debate. The two negative speakers must communicate with each other to decide what arguments to run.

Cooperation goes beyond the affirmative and negative team. Many times there is more research work to be done than one team can do. On a debate squad everyone works together to do the research on negative. The resources are then pooled and used by everyone on the squad. The same can be done in a classroom setting. Research assignments can be divided and shared. The ability to work well with others is a valuable life skill. When we cooperate and work with others it is often possible to find a compromise to many problems. Several minds working together may lead to solutions that are more advantageous than those to be found in isolation.

2

The Mechanics of Debate

The first time you participate in a sports activity, you may find the game to be slow-going and difficult. Often the terminology is strange, the rules are new, and the territory is unfamiliar. But after you become familiar with the concept behind the game and its rules, you often find that it becomes easier and enjoyable to you. In a sense debate is also a game, difficult at first, but one that becomes easier with practice. In this chapter, you will be introduced to the fundamentals of debate. After you understand them, you will be able to go on, in following chapters, to use them in the planning and preparing and delivering of arguments. To do this, you will need to understand the following key terms:

burden of proof	prima facie
constructive	problem area
flow sheet	rebuttal
presumption	topicality

Debate is made up of many different parts. They include terminology, ideas, and processes. Debaters must know and understand these elements. In this chapter, we will take our first look at the problem area, the proposition, affirmative, negative, and flow sheeting. These are the basic elements of debate.

THE PROBLEM AREA

Before we can define proposition, we need to understand the term *problem area.* A problem area is a general question of some concern to a community or group of people. Problem areas might be water pollution, poverty, national defense, or medical care. Each of these problem areas is too broad and vague to lead to a profitable discussion or debate. From the problem area we need a question on which to focus our attention. In the area of medical care, the question might be "Should adequate medical care be guaranteed?" But we are still dealing with a broad subject area. For whom should medical care be provided? At what cost should medical care be provided? What type of medical care should be provided? A more specific question might be worded "Should medical care for catastrophic illnesses be provided for everyone?" In debate the question would then be put in the form of a proposition: "Resolved: That the federal government should guarantee medical care for those with catastrophic illnesses."

ACTIVITIES
1. Look around you at issues of concern in your school and community. Identify one problem in your school and one in your community. Phrase the problems as questions. Do they need to be narrowed in scope? Why would these problem areas be of interest for debate? Would it be possible to research the problems?

2. Repeat Activity 1 by identifying problem areas in the national and international communities.

PROPOSITION

Most debate propositions present a clear and important choice. The function of the proposition is to provide focus for discussion and debate. The three types of propositions (fact, value, and policy) are discussed in Chapter 4.

Characteristics of a Proposition
A proposition must possess certain characteristics. They include significance, controversy, a single idea, debatability, and durability.

Significance
The problem to be debated should be significant. It should affect a large number of people around the country or even around the world. The problem of how to provide jobs for all employable United States citizens would be the basis for a significant proposition because the problem affects most Americans. Inflation, access to medical care, toxic wastes, pollution, national defense, world hunger, and the proliferation of nuclear weapons are all significant problem areas and would be potential candidates for debate propositions. However, city taxes, county jails, state lotteries, or fire codes would normally not be appropriate for debate propositions. They lack significance in that they affect only a limited number of people. This does not mean that such problem areas are *never* appropriate for debate. There may

be times when the situation calls for debating an issue that is limited in scope. This is often the case in *audience debates.* An audience debate is a debate before a group of people with no specific background in debate. A limited problem area is usually chosen because it is of more interest to the specific audience and will likely have a greater impact.

QUESTIONS FOR DISCUSSION

1. Are there times when it is appropriate to debate a proposition more limited in scope? Why?

2. Name three problem areas that would be of interest to *your* school's student body. Are they significant to people who are not associated with your school?

Controversy

A proposition is debatable only if it is controversial. That is, there must be a difference of opinion or a conflict of interest regarding the proposition. Often, in propositions of fact there is no dispute, no controversy, and therefore no debate. For example, the proposition "Resolved: That the Constitution provides for a separation of church and state" is not controversial. It is a fact that can be verified. However, the proposition "Resolved: That President John F. Kennedy was killed by a single assassin" is a proposition of fact, but it is open to a great deal of controversy.

QUESTION FOR DISCUSSION

1. In the two example propositions given above, why is one debatable while the other is not?

A single idea

A debate proposition should contain only one idea. To prepare and argue effectively, the debater must be able to focus on a single problem area. The proposition "Resolved: That the United States should become energy independent and work to purify the air and water" presents two subjects for argument. The first is energy independence and the second is pollution control. To try to debate both subjects in the same round will lead to poorly developed arguments and a great deal of confusion. Each should be debated as a separate proposition.

ACTIVITY

1. The example proposition given above contains two ideas. Rewrite it as two propositions, each with a single idea.

Debatability

The proposition should be stated as impartially as possible. Emotional language that would color the debate should be avoided. Use of emotional language can give the affirmative or the negative an unfair advantage. For example, "Resolved: That rehabilitation programs should be established for hardened, dangerous criminals" is stated with a slant to the negative. The wording implies that rehabilitation would be difficult, if not impossible.

The proposition should be worded so that it does not favor the affirmative or the negative. For example, "Resolved: That all United States citizens have a right to clean drinking water" places a heavy burden on the negative. It is not a reasonable negative position to argue that citizens do not have a *right* to clean drinking water. A more debatable proposition would be "Resolved: That the federal government should establish a comprehensive national policy to protect the quality of drinking water in the United States." This wording provides a better balance of issues and arguments for the affirmative and the negative.

QUESTIONS FOR DISCUSSION

1. Why is it important for a proposition to be debatable?

2. In the two examples given above, explain why each is not debatable as originally written.

3. In the example above on rehabilitation programs, how would you reword the proposition to make it debatable?

Durability Will the problem continue to exist during the time period for the debates? For example, "Resolved: That students should be allowed to leave campus during their free class periods" would be a risky topic for debate if the school administration is considering such a proposal for implementation. The affirmative will have little to debate if the administration adopts the proposal during the course of the semester. A proposition should be of interest, but its adoption in the immediate future should be unlikely.

QUESTIONS FOR DISCUSSION

1. What are the five characteristics of a *proposition*?

2. Why is durability a necessary characteristic of a proposition?

ACTIVITIES

1. Each of the propositions below contains a flaw. Identify which of the five characteristics it does not meet. Explain why.

Resolved: That the military draft should be reinstated with registration at a student's local high school.

Resolved: That the federal government should establish comprehensive security guidelines for United States airports to make them safe.

Resolved: That the federal government should increase social welfare programs in the current budget.

Resolved: That city governments should establish a program to improve the collection of parking fines.

Resolved: That enrollment in elementary schools is rising.

Resolved: That fresh vegetable prices fluctuate with the growing seasons.

Resolved: That the federal government should redesign the tax structure to tax citizens equally and use a significant portion of the tax dollars to improve the educational system.

Resolved: That the federal government should establish a comprehensive program to provide medical care for all Americans.

2. After you have identified the flaws in the propositions in Activity 1, rewrite them into a correct proposition.

3. Write three propositions you would be interested in debating. They can involve school policy, local policy, state regulations, or federal issues. Explain how one of the propositions meets the five characteristics of a proposition.

AFFIRMATIVE

It is the job of the affirmative team to argue for the adoption of the resolution (proposition). Remember that the proposition calls for a change to be made in the present system. A debate resolution is usually open to a number of interpretations. On the topic "Resolved: That the federal government should establish a comprehensive program to significantly increase the energy independence of the United States," possible interpretations would include stripmining of coal, oil imports, nuclear power, solar power, the Alaskan pipeline, etc. Any of these would be an appropriate topic for debate. The affirmative decides which area of the proposition it wishes to discuss. This is referred to as the *affirmative case.* The affirmative case is the position to be developed by the affirmative throughout the debate. The structure of the affirmative case includes justification for change, a plan, and the advantages of the plan. The affirmative case may be organized in a number of ways (see Chapter 7). The term "case" is sometimes confusing, because in debate the word "case" can be divided into two basic parts (1) justification for change (which is called the *case side*) and (2) a plan for implementing that change (which is called the *plan side*). The types of affirmative case structure and the obligations and duties of each are discussed in detail in Chapter 7.

QUESTIONS FOR DISCUSSION

1. Does the affirmative argue for or against the proposition?

2. The area the affirmative chooses to debate is developed into what is known as the _____.

3. What are the three components of the affirmative case structure?

PRESUMPTION

Presumption means that the policy now in effect should remain in effect. The feeling is that the values that led to the current policy will continue to exist and that what is currently accepted as true will continue to be accepted as true. Thus, the affirmative side, which always argues for change, is obligated to *prove* that change is necessary. Presumption usually favors the negative. The negative generally argues that the current state of affairs is adequate and in no need of major change. An example of presumption can be found in the American judicial system, where a person is presumed innocent until proven guilty.

At one time segregated schools were legal. This was the present system. Many thought or presumed it worked well. Changes in values, conditions, and policies created an environment for a change. The present system was questioned and debated. Then, the U.S. Supreme Court ruled that segregation was unconstitutional, and a change was ordered. Values, conditions, and policies now set up an environment for a program of integration. With these changes in values, conditions and policies the present system is now one of integration. This includes funding and programs geared to encourage and expand integration.

In debate the affirmative must prove that there is reason to change the present system. When this is not adequately proven, the negative wins the debate.

QUESTIONS FOR DISCUSSION

1. Does the affirmative or the negative begin the debate with *presumption*? Why?

2. Why is presumption a very important element in criminal law in the United States? What are the implications in nonlegal areas, such as politics and debate?

BURDEN OF PROOF

The affirmative must provide sufficient reason for adopting the proposition. This is called the *burden of proof.* It always rests with the affirmative team. In a court of law it is the prosecution's responsibility to prove beyond a reasonable doubt that the accused committed the crime. In a debate round, the affirmative takes on the role of the prosecution and must prove that a change is needed. If the affirmative does not present a significant justification for change, it does not fulfill its burden of proof.

Although the negative must prove what it asserts, it is never in the position of trying to prove that the proposition should be adopted. Even if the negative agreed that the present system should be changed, it would never argue in support of the specific change suggested in the debate proposition. If it did, there would be no debate.

QUESTIONS FOR DISCUSSION

1. In debate the burden of proof rests with the _____. Why?

2. If the burden of proof is not upheld by the prosecutor in a court of law, the defendant will be found innocent of the charges. When the burden of proof is not upheld in debate, what is the result?

THE PRIMA-FACIE CASE

Prima facie is a French term meaning "on face value" or "at first sight." The affirmative in debate must present a case that is complete "at first sight." Debate operates under the assumption that the affirmative can overcome presumption and thus meet the burden of proof only by presenting a prima-facie case. Thus, the affirmative must do more than state a justification, describe a plan, and list its advantages. The affirmative must support each of these issues with enough evidence and analysis to make a case both qualitatively and quantitatively. The case must be established strongly enough in the mind of the judge to justify a favorable decision. It must be strong enough to stand alone until it is weakened or refuted by the negative.

A prima-facie case must stem directly from the proposition and give good and sufficient reason for adopting the proposition. In debate, a prima-facie case is the minimal argument required to support the proposition without refutation. Unless the affirmative team establishes a prima-facie case, it cannot win a debate. Technically, if the affirmative does not establish a prima-facie case, the negative does not need to reply to affirmative arguments. However, most negative teams will refute any case that appears to the average person to be a prima-facie case. The specific approaches that the affirmative may take to develop a prima-facie case are developed in Chapter 7.

QUESTIONS FOR DISCUSSION

1. What does *prima facie* mean?

2. In order to present a prima-facie case, what must the affirmative do?

3. What happens if the affirmative does not present a prima-facie case?

NEGATIVE

The negative team responds to the affirmative by attacking and destroying the arguments. This is called *refutation.* Remember, the affirmative chooses the specific case area to be debated in the round. As a result, it is able to prepare many of its arguments well in advance. Because the affirmative team usually argues the same case round after round, it becomes very experienced at defending the case. The negative, on the other hand, may find itself refuting a number of different cases. If the negative debates four rounds, it may have to refute anywhere from one to four affirmative cases. For example, on the energy topic the negative might have to debate against a stripmining case in round one, an oil imports case in round two, a nuclear power case in round three, and a solar power case in round four. With each proposition, there will usually be a number of general points the negative can prepare to be used against a number of affirmative cases. However, the negative also must try to anticipate the specific arguments of each case and prepare specific refutations for each argument. In the debate round the negative learns to think quickly, improvise, and apply the appropriate negative arguments to the specific affirmative case being presented.

The negative refutes the affirmative case in three general areas. First, the negative may want to deny that the affirmative harm exists. The affirmative *harm* is an undesirable impact caused by the present system. Harm exists where needs are denied or suffering or loss of life is created. The negative can deny the harm by challenging the affirmative measurement of harm or by indicating that the harm outlined is one assumed by choice and therefore should not be considered a harm.

Second, the negative may argue that adopting the proposition will not solve (meet) the affirmative harm. The negative will argue that the present system is capable of solving the problem, that the present system has recently adopted programs that will solve the problem, or that recent changes in conditions unrelated to the harm will solve the problem in the future. Essentially, the negative is challenging the affirmative's *inherency* (justification for change).

Third, the negative may want to attack the affirmative plan. This is done by demonstrating that the plan can be *circumvented,* does not take into account outside factors which could affect the plan, or has an internal flaw. The negative might show that the affirmative plan will not meet the needs outlined by the affirmative. The negative might also maintain that adopting the affirmative plan will result in negative side effects and that the *disadvantages* will outweigh the advantages gained by the affirmative plan.

The negative needs to win only *one* argument (harm, inherency, plan meet need, or disadvantages) to win the debate. Negative approaches and strategies are discussed in greater detail in Chapter 8.

QUESTIONS FOR DISCUSSION

1. What are the three general areas in which the negative can refute the affirmative case?

2. How does the negative argue that the affirmative harm does not exist?

3. Generally, what does it mean to challenge the affirmative's *inherency*?

4. What types of arguments does the negative make to challenge the affirmative plan? Define each.

HOW TO TAKE A FLOW

The most basic tactic in refutation and rebuttal is to know and remember what has been said during the round. Surprisingly, many debaters simply don't listen carefully to the arguments of their opponents and, as a result, miss many of the subtleties of the case and often misinterpret the opponent's arguments. The first step, then, is to develop a system for taking notes that will guarantee that the debater hears the arguments and later can report them accurately to the judge.

"*Flow sheeting*" is the term that many debaters use to describe the process of taking notes during a debate. The goal is to follow the flow of the debate and accurately to record all of the principal arguments of the debaters involved in the round. Typically, notes are taken on two large sheets of paper. Many debaters use legal-size pads (or pre-printed flow sheets*). Most speakers partition the pad ahead of time and allow one section for each speech in the debate (see Debate Flows, pp. 16–17).

The important thing is to accurately record what is said during the debate, and most speakers develop abbreviation systems that allow them to record information very quickly. Words that you hear a lot in debates should have a symbol in your system. For example, increase can be an arrow pointing up; decrease, an arrow pointing down. Every person's system will be different, but without some kind of system you will not be able to flow efficiently. Remember it takes a lot longer to write out the word "topicality" than to simply mark a capital "T." Developing a system like this will also help you take notes in classes. If a long word is used that you do not have a symbol for, you should either write only a syllable or two (enough so that you will recognize the word later) or you can leave out the vowels. For example "professional" would be written down as "profess" or as "prfssnl."

Use an "X" to indicate the use of evidence. Finally, when you write an argument down you should join it, with a line, to the argument it is answering. This is what gives the flow sheet its name. Many people find that it helps to flow the different sides in different colors; red for negative, blue for affirmative. It takes time and lots of practice to become an accurate flow-er but successful debaters know it is worth the effort.

ACTIVITIES

1. Create a list of abbreviations and symbols that could be used for note taking.

2. Practice using these abbreviations and symbols listening to class lectures, the nightly news or the radio.

*Large pads, pre-printed in black and red to distinguish affirmative and negative entries, are available from National Textbook Company, Lincolnwood, Illinois.

Affirmative Case Flow

First Affirmative Constructive	First Negative Constructive	Second Affirmative Constructive	First Negative Rebuttal	First Affirmative Rebuttal	Second Negative Rebuttal	Second Affirmative Rebuttal
Observ: U.S. is oil oriented — x	I. Researching tech. — x 2. ∅ lock into I policy	1. Tech. avail. now for hydrogen 2. Other tech. not avail. yet	Still experimental Plan wld. stop research	Why not meet	1. Not flexible policy	1. e. indep. 2. 50% 3. can deve. alts.
I. Aff. ↑ e. indep. A. Imports sign. — x x	I. A. 1. Not sign. — x x 2. Domestic drilling ↑ — x	→ 50% and ↑ — x x 1. Not amt. needed 2. Supplies ↓ — x	Oil down 1980s — x No incentive to keep drilling — x	Does not solve problem	2. Oil demand ↓ — x	1. 50% of need 2. 95% F.F.
B. Imports are harmful — x x x x	B. 1. No OPEC harms — x x x x 2. Prices ∅ harmful — x x x 3. Trade surplus — x	1. Unemployment — x x 2. For. pol. — x 3. Trade deficit — x 4. Vunerable to shortages — x	1. Prices frozen — x 2. Causes not harm 3. Reserves can handle — x x		3. OPEC harms ∅ proven – have oil reserve	1. 50% 2. Demand
C. Hydrogen ↑ e. indep. 1. Autos — x 2. Home heating — x	C. 1. Researching now 2. Ready for use soon — x 3. Govt. funding — x	1. No capital outlays 2. P.S. relies on oil 3. F.F. = 95% — x	1. Govt. funding 2. R&D — x 3. 7 projects 4. Can be ready	Take huge capital outlays	4. Research on hydro-gen with govt. funds	1. not enough 2. not competitive 3. Techn. exists
II. Aff. saves lives from poll. control A. Auto exhaust — x B. Death and suffering — x C. Hydrogen 1. Feasible — x 2. Non-polluting — x	II. 1. Studies overstate 2. Counterstudies — x 3. Auto regulation — x 4. Auto poll ∅ sign. — x	1. Just fact update 2. CO_2 problem — x x → not save lives — x	Aff. burden 1. overstated 2. EPA control — x 3. Cut ½ in future — x	Not NO_x — x	5. Only 50% of harm → causes pollution	

Plan Flow

Affirmative Plan	Second Negative Constructive	First Affirmative Rebuttal	Second Negative Rebuttal	Second Affirmative Rebuttal
1. Board - Dpt. Interior	PMA 1. No training for people	1. No proof 2. No harm to change over	1. No specifics 2. Not know what's going on	→ Can provide
2. Mandates A. Production 1. Hydrogen 2. Prod. alloc. quotas	2. Not prov. e. A. Yrs. to convert B. Tech. problems 1. Ineff X	Within 4 yrs. ——— X Have hybrids now X	Years to convert X Ineffective X	1. Feasible X 2. Hybrids 3. can store
B. Conservation 1. Home heating 2. Cars 3. Gaseous metal hydrates	2. Costly X 3. Pollution X 4. Storage X	No massive prod.; cheap. Can take care of		
C. Regulate imports	DAs 1. Endanger America A. ↑ use B. Hydrogen causes embrittlement – small breaks X	No problem X →	What use rate? What tech.?	1. Solve embrittlement 2. Hybrids 3. Texas evidence 4. Hydrogen ∅ poll.
3. Storage & transp. –pipelines	C. Impact explosion or fire X X			
4. Funding –liqu. taxes –diversion –cut def.	2. Eco. harm A. Costly 1. Massive investment			

5. Enfor.	2. Compare to F.F.
	 X
	B. Inflation
	 X
	 X
	 X
		1. Not total hydrogen
		2. $40B a yr. over
		  20 yrs.
			1. not all across nation
			2. Never show exact
			  amt. of OPEC
			3. Costly compared
			  to F.F.
				1. Import ½ oil
				2. Cheaper than gas
				3. Funding minimal

	C. Harms
	 1. Unemployment
	  X
	 2. Investment hurt
	  X
	  X			

3

Debate Formats and Speaker Responsibilities

Whether the event is the Indianapolis 500, the Olympic ice hockey finals or the Super Bowl, you can be sure that all winning team members know exactly what their roles are and how they fit into the overall team plan. Organization, planning and teamwork are essential to winning. Like other activities, successful debate depends on each team member playing a particular position with special responsibilities. Speech order, length, and duties are determined before the debate begins. In this chapter we will look at speaker responsibilities and the various debate formats. After reading this chapter, you should understand the following key terms:

constructive speech
cross-examination debate
Lincoln-Douglas debate

preparation time
rebuttal speech
speaker responsibilities
standard debate

DEBATE FORMATS

Three formats are popular in academic debate. The first is the *traditional* or *standard debate* format. This format is used most often by beginning debaters. The second is the *cross-examination debate* format, which is used by most tournaments at the high school and college level. The third is *Lincoln-Douglas debate* format. This is a two-person debate format named in honor of the two famous debaters who used this format—Abraham Lincoln and Stephen Douglas.

Standard Debate Format

The *standard debate* format was used by high schools and colleges almost exclusively until the mid–1970s. The standard debate format consists of two types of speeches: the *constructive speech* and the *rebuttal speech.* The constructive speech ranges from 8 to 10 minutes in length and presents the major points made by each team. The rebuttal speech is 4 to 5 minutes in length and follows the constructive speeches. The rebuttal is used to refute and/or extend major arguments.

During the seventies, cross-examination debate began to grow in popularity and slowly replaced the standard debate format at tournaments. The format is still used today at many novice tournaments (tournaments for beginning debaters). Debaters use this format while learning the basics of debate. Once they have mastered the basic skills, debaters learn cross-examination skills and move on to participate in cross-examination debate.

Standard Debate Format

	High School	College
First Affirmative Constructive Speech	8 minutes	10 minutes
First Negative Constructive Speech	8 minutes	10 minutes
Second Affirmative Constructive Speech	8 minutes	10 minutes
Second Negative Constructive Speech	8 minutes	10 minutes
First Negative Rebuttal Speech	4 minutes	5 minutes
First Affirmative Rebuttal Speech	4 minutes	5 minutes
Second Negative Rebuttal Speech	4 minutes	5 minutes
Second Affirmative Rebuttal Speech	4 minutes	5 minutes

Cross-Examination Debate Format

Cross-examination debate first appeared during the 1930s. Considered experimental, innovative, and creative, cross-examination debate was becoming the preferred debate format by the mid–1970s. Cross-examination debate is similar to standard debate with the addition of question periods (cross-examination) after each constructive speech. The question periods provide an opportunity for direct confrontation between opposing members of the two teams.

Cross-Examination Debate Format

	High School	College
First Affirmative Constructive Speech	8 minutes	10 minutes
Negative Cross-examination of First Affirmative Constructive Speaker	3 minutes	3 minutes
First Negative Constructive Speech	8 minutes	10 minutes
Affirmative Cross-examination of First Negative Constructive Speaker	3 minutes	3 minutes
Second Affirmative Constructive Speech	8 minutes	10 minutes
Negative Cross-examination of Second Affirmative Constructive Speaker	3 minutes	3 minutes
Second Negative Constructive Speech	8 minutes	10 minutes
Affirmative Cross-examination of Second Negative Constructive Speaker	3 minutes	3 minutes
First Negative Rebuttal Speech	4 minutes	5 minutes
First Affirmative Rebuttal Speech	4 minutes	5 minutes
Second Negative Rebuttal Speech	4 minutes	5 minutes
Second Affirmative Rebuttal Speech	4 minutes	5 minutes

Lincoln-Douglas Debate Format

Lincoln-Douglas debate involves only two participants (one on each side) instead of four, as in standard and cross-examination debate. A value proposition is used in place of a policy proposition. The aim is to be persuasive before an audience with an emphasis on analysis, as opposed to evidence. The National Forensics League established Lincoln-Douglas debate as a national event.

The total speaking time allocated to each side for speaking and for cross-examination is the same, but the time blocks are not the same. The affirmative has less time to establish its constructive case than does the negative, which allows the negative to respond to specific arguments introduced by the affirmative and to offer additional negative materials and issues in the first speech without having to use a fast delivery. The affirmative has an equal amount of time but it is allocated differently. In addition, the affirmative debater speaks three times. The negative debater speaks only twice. The fact that there is more cross-examination time in proportion to the total debate time means that cross-examination skills become proportionately more important to the outcome of the debate. You will notice that the total amount of time necessary for a debate using the Lincoln-Douglas format is only one-half that required by the standard or cross-examination debate format.

Lincoln-Douglas Debate Format

Affirmative Constructive Speech	6 minutes
Negative Cross-examination of Affirmative	3 minutes
Negative Constructive Speech	7 minutes
Affirmative Cross-examination of Negative	3 minutes
Affirmative Rebuttal Speech	4 minutes
Negative Rebuttal Speech	6 minutes
Affirmative Rebuttal Speech	3 minutes

QUESTIONS FOR DISCUSSION

1. What are the differences among standard, cross-examination, and Lincoln-Douglas debate?

2. What do you think are the advantages of using cross-examination debate?

PREPARATION TIME

To some degree, debate is an *extemporaneous* speaking activity. Entire speeches are not written before the debate begins (with the exception of the first affirmative constructive speech). To be an effective debater one must take some time to organize and put materials together before standing up to speak. The time used between speeches for preparation is known as *preparation time* (prep time). Since it would be unreasonable to allow limitless amounts of time for preparation in a round, time limits are set for each round or tournament, by its organizers. Three types of preparation time rules will be discussed here.

One-Minute (Two-Minute) Rule

This rule applies to the individual speaker. Each speaker is allowed one (or two) minutes to prepare a single speech. Preparation means jotting down final notes, gathering materials, and getting to the podium to speak. For example, when the first affirmative constructive speaker finishes speaking and sits down, the preparation time for the first negative constructive speaker begins. In one (or two) minutes the first negative constructive speaker is expected to be ready to speak. If the speaker takes longer than the one (or two) minutes the additional time is subtracted from his or her speaking time.

Eight-Minute Rule

The eight-minute rule is the preparation time rule most commonly used in debate rounds. The rule applies to the affirmative and the negative as a team. Each team is given a total of eight minutes' preparation time to use as it wishes. Preparation time is calculated from the time one speaker sits down until the next speaker begins speaking. The elapsed time is recorded by the timekeeper (or judge, if there is no timekeeper). Each team is informed as each minute of preparation time elapses. No rule governs how each team allocates its preparation time. For example, the negative might use four minutes before the first negative constructive speech, one minute before the second negative constructive speech, one minute before the first negative rebuttal speech, and two minutes before the second negative rebuttal speech. The affirmative may wish to use most of its preparation time before the first affirmative rebuttal speech so that important speech can be carefully planned. When a team has used the full eight minutes, any additional preparation time is subtracted from subsequent speaking time for that team. Unused preparation time cannot be saved for another debate round. Any unused preparation time is simply lost time.

There are two variations of this rule. They are the five-minute rule and the ten-minute. The procedure is the same, but the total preparation time for each team is shorter or longer. Which time frame is used is left up to the discretion of the tournament director.

Lincoln-Douglas Debate

In Lincoln-Douglas debate, each debater is allowed a total of three minutes' preparation time during the debate. The rules for using this prep time are the same as for the eight-minute rule.

SPEAKER DUTIES AND RESPONSIBILITIES

An important first step in learning to debate is developing an understanding of each speaker's duties and responsibilities. They are the blueprint for a debate round, the rules of the game. Arguments are presented, developed, and critiqued during the constructive speeches. These are followed by rebuttal speeches that are half as long. The purpose of these speeches is to extend arguments and to summarize the affirmative and negative positions.

Each debate begins with the first affirmative constructive speech. The first affirmative speaker claims that the resolution should be supported. The first negative constructive speech follows with a refutation of the arguments (contentions) that were presented by the first affirmative. The second affirmative speaker then attempts to rebuild the affirmative case (redevelop the first affirmative arguments). The second negative constructive speech poses objections to the affirmative plan (the affirmative solution to the problem presented by the affirmative).

Speaker positions alter somewhat in rebuttals. Rebuttal speeches begin with the first negative rebuttal and alternate until the second affirmative has the last speech in the debate. The first negative rebuttal argues against the responses developed by the second affirmative constructive speaker. The first affirmative rebuttalist must respond to all the negative arguments (the second negative constructive arguments and first negative rebuttal extensions). This can be as much as fifteen minutes of negative speaking time. The first affirmative rebuttal is viewed by many as the most difficult speech in the entire debate.

Speaker Order and Speaker Responsibilities

Speaker Order	Speaker Responsibilities
First Affirmative Constructive Speech	Presents reasons for change (contentions or advantages) and a solution.
First Negative Constructive Speech	Challenges affirmative's definition of terms, topicality, and refutation of affirmative's contentions or advantage.
Second Affirmative Constructive Speech	Rebuilds the affirmative case, refutes major negative arguments, and extends remaining affirmative arguments.
Second Negative Constructive Speech	Presents objections to the affirmative's plan. These include plan workability, plan solvency, and disadvantages.
First Negative Rebuttal Speech	Refutes, extends, and develops the case arguments introduced by the second affirmative.
First Affirmative Rebuttal Speech	Responds to all negative arguments (the second negative constructive arguments and first negative rebuttal extensions).
Second Negative Rebuttal Speech	Extends negative arguments on case and plan. Selectivity is crucial. These arguments are usually labelled "voting" issues.
Second Affirmative Rebuttal Speech	Answers negative's objections extended in the second negative rebuttal and re-establishes the affirmative case.

The last two rebuttal speeches sum up final positions. The second negative must select a few important objections to extend. Because there is not time to argue and extend everything, it is necessary to be selective. The second affirmative rebuttalist has an obligation to answer the negative objections extended in the second negative rebuttal and then reestablish the affirmative case.

QUESTIONS FOR DISCUSSION

1. What is a *constructive* speech?

2. What is a *rebuttal* speech?

First Affirmative Constructive Speech

The *first affirmative constructive speech* is usually all-inclusive. It includes contentions, plan, advantages. Thus, all of the affirmative reasons for change are set out at the beginning of the debate. This leads to better development of arguments, clearer definition of issues, and a greater opportunity for both teams to analyze and extend arguments.

Strategy: To present the strongest possible case for the proposition and to leave the affirmative in a strong offensive position.

Duties:
1. Give a brief, pleasant introduction that capsulizes the affirmative's approach.
2. Give a statement of the resolution (proposition).
3. Define the key terms of the resolution (proposition).
4. Present the affirmative's justification for a change. (In the need case this is the need or harm contention. Present the affirmative justification for comparative harms in the comparative advantage case. See pages 81–83).
5. Present the affirmative's plan (proposed solution to the problem presented).
6. Present the advantages of the affirmative's plan.
7. Give a brief summary of the affirmative's case.

The order in which 4, 5, and 6 are presented depends on the type of affirmative case being argued. (In the need case the order of presentation would be 4, 5, and 6, while in the comparative advantage case the order of presentation would be 5, 6, and then 4. See pages 81–83.)

Outline for First Affirmative Constructive Speech
I. Introduction
II. Statement of the resolution
III. Definition of terms (sometimes these are defined by the plan)
IV. Inherency
V. Significance
VI. Presentation of the plan
VII. Solvency of the plan (need case)
VIII. Advantages of the plan (comparative advantage case). This is optional when presenting the need case.

QUESTIONS FOR DISCUSSION

1. What are the parts of a first affirmative constructive speech?

2. What is the strategy behind the first affirmative constructive speech?

3. What elements should be in the first affirmative constructive speech?

First Negative Constructive Speech

The *first negative constructive speech* is in direct response to the first affirmative constructive speech. Here the negative must decide if it agrees with the affirmative definition of terms and choice of topic area. The negative must decide at this juncture what its position as a team will be against the affirmative case.

Strategy: To maintain the validity of the present system, to take the offensive away from the affirmative, and to expand the debate beyond the arguments presented in the first affirmative constructive speech.

Duties:
1. Give a brief introduction and explanation of the negative's philosophy in the debate.
2. Provide the negative's organization for analyzing the affirmative's arguments.
3. Challenge the affirmative's definition of terms. This usually requires both explanation and evidence. However, when need be it can be done with explanation alone.
4. Challenge the affirmative's topicality. This is a challenge of the specific affirmative case area. For example, an affirmative team that argues for educating school children about AIDS and its causes on the topic "Resolved: That the federal government should establish minimum educational standards for elementary and secondary schools in the United States" may be challenged on topicality. Does educating our children about AIDS fall within the scope (or intent) of such a resolution? The issue would definitely be debatable.
5. Defend the present system by summarizing its aims and effectiveness in meeting its goals.
6. Argue that the affirmative team has not presented an adequate justification for changing the present system.
7. Give a brief summary of the negative's position in the debate.

It is not necessary for the first negative to go through all seven steps. However, if the negative plans to challenge the affirmative's definition of terms or topicality, it should be done in the first negative constructive speech.

Outline for First Negative Constructive Speech
I. Introduction and statement of the negative philosophy. It should state the negative position with regard to the particular affirmative case being run in the round and should constitute a negative constructive argument that can be an issue later in the debate.
II. Definition of terms. If the negative is going to disagree with the affirmative's definitions, this is the time and place for it. The disagreement should be developed as an argument. There should be counter evidence or authorities to support the negative position. How the definition affects the affirmative case should be shown.
III. Topicality. If the negative is going to challenge the affirmative's topicality, this is the time and place for the argument. Care should be taken to explain carefully why the affirmative case does not fall within the bounds of the resolution.

IV. Each refutation should be structured. The following format will serve for each point:
    A. State the affirmative point to be refuted. Use the affirmative's labels.
    B. State your position relative to the affirmative contention.
    C. Present evidence for the negative point.
    D. Explain the impact on the affirmative case. What damage does your point do to the affirmative case?
    E. Restate your position.
V. A restatement of the negative philosophy or a summary of the negative impact on the affirmative case overall can make a strong appeal for the negative position.

Structuring and labeling your arguments is important. If your arguments are not easy to identify, they will be lost later in the debate. Use numerical and alphabetical designations to keep the substructure clear.

QUESTIONS FOR DISCUSSION

1. What is the strategy for the first negative constructive speech?

2. What are the issues the first negative should raise in this constructive speech?

Second Affirmative Constructive Speech

The *second affirmative constructive speech* has three primary purposes: (1) to reestablish the affirmative position in the debate, (2) to refute the major arguments presented by the first negative speaker, and (3) to extend affirmative arguments and present any remaining constructive materials for the affirmative.

Strategy: To uphold the affirmative's burden of proof, to remain on the offensive, and to narrow the range of arguments.

Duties:
1. Give a brief introduction.
2. Prove that the affirmative case justifies the topic by reestablishing the affirmative definition of terms and topicality, if challenged.
3. Reestablish the affirmative justification for change.
4. Prove that the harm exists, is significant, and is likely to grow worse in the future if nothing is done.
5. Demonstrate that the harm is caused by the present system or that the advantages are unique to the affirmative plan.
6. Review affirmative arguments that have not been attacked up to this point.
7. Provide a brief summary.

The second affirmative constructive speaker should be ready to refute anything the first negative constructive speaker brings up. Where possible, the second affirmative constructive speaker should draw negative arguments back into the affirmative case structure. The second affirmative constructive speaker may also present additional advantages. However, this should not be done at the expense of an adequate case defense.

Outline for Second Affirmative Constructive Speech

I. Overview of the debate thus far, showing the relationship between the affirmative case and the negative philosophy (introduction).

II. Defense of the definition of terms and/or topicality, if necessary.

III. Reestablishment of the affirmative inherency (harm or advantage and its significance). Answer negative refutation.

IV. Attack any negative constructive materials. When possible, use affirmative contentions to refute the negative philosophy or negative arguments defending the present system.

V. Summarize, emphasizing arguments dropped by the negative and arguments being carried by the affirmative.

If the second affirmative constructive speaker is going to introduce additional advantages, it can be done in one of two places. Advantages may be introduced after the introduction or after answering all negative attacks and before giving a final affirmative summary. While it is useful to have additional advantages in the second affirmative constructive speech, it should never be done at the expense of an adequate response to the arguments raised by the negative. It is of little value to win an additional advantage if one loses inherency because of an inadequate response.

QUESTIONS FOR DISCUSSIONS

1. What are the three purposes of the second affirmative constructive speech?

2. What is the strategy of the second affirmative constructive speech?

3. Should the second affirmative constructive speaker try to introduce additional advantages? Where should these be placed in the speech?

Second Negative Constructive Speech

Traditionally, the *second negative constructive speech* deals with the affirmative plan. There may be times when a new argument on case (the justification for change) needs to be developed. However, this should be done only occasionally. The primary purpose of the second negative constructive speech is to deal with three issues: (1) plan workability, (2) plan solvency, and (3) plan disadvantages.

Strategy: To outline plan workability and solvency problems and disadvantages to adopting the affirmative plan.

Duties:

1. Give an introduction that outlines what the second negative speaker plans to do in this speech. This is important because the structure of this speech departs from the affirmative case structure. One should be laying out a road map for everyone to follow for plan objections.

2. Show why the affirmative's proposal is unworkable or impractical. This might involve three or four separate and numbered arguments.

3. Show why the affirmative's plan will not solve the problems of the present system outlined by the affirmative on case (the justification for change).

4. Detail the disadvantages of the affirmative's plan. This might involve as many as five or six specific harmful side effects of the plan. It is better to have two or three well-developed disadvantages than six poorly developed ones. Disadvantages should be presented with supporting evidence.

5. Give a very brief conclusion. This may involve contrasting the advantages (minimized by the first negative constructive speaker) with the disadvantages and demonstrate (when possible) that the disadvantages outweigh the advantages offered by the affirmative.

The *extension* (or continuation) of case arguments should be handled by the first negative rebuttal speaker. Always keep in mind that the second negative constructive speech is the first speech of the negative block. It is followed immediately by the first negative rebuttal. Solvency and workability arguments may be proven in some cases by the use of explanation. When evidence is available it should be used. However, solvency and workability arguments are usually arguments of logic. Disadvantages, on the other hand, require evidence to support them. A disadvantage should be developed with as much care as one develops an affirmative harm contention or advantage.

Outline for Second Negative Constructive Speech
I. Introduction with references to the negative philosophy presented by the first negative constructive speaker. A brief outline of intentions should be included.
II. Workability. Attacks on specific *elements* of the affirmative plan should be presented here. For example, if the affirmative needs $50 million for its plan and is using a cigarette tax to raise the money, then the negative might argue that this tax will not raise enough money.
III. Solvency. Demonstrations that the affirmative's plan is incapable of meeting the need or achieving the advantages claimed should be given here.
IV. Disadvantages. Develop here any and all attacks to demonstrate that even if the affirmative plan could solve the need or achieve the advantage, it would create disadvantages that would offset the plan's desirability. Examples of disadvantages might include unemployment, decreases in military spending, starvation in third world countries (limiting agricultural exports), or pollution (from stripmining coal to gain more energy). When you are developing disadvantages it is important to illustrate their general significance and their uniqueness to the affirmative plan. You need to show why the affirmative plan causes these disadvantages but the present system does not.

QUESTIONS FOR DISCUSSION

1. What is the primary focus of the second negative constructive speech?

2. What should be the strategy of the second negative constructive speech?

3. Solvency and workability arguments are usually arguments of _____.

First Negative Rebuttal Speech

The *first negative rebuttal speech* is the first of the rebuttal speeches. It is delivered right after the second negative constructive speech. The second negative constructive speech and the first negative rebuttal speech are often referred to as the *negative block.* When structured with care the negative block can have a significant impact on the affirmative case. First negative rebuttalist will want to refute, extend, and develop the case arguments that were introduced by the second affirmative constructive speaker. Because this speech is half the time of the first negative constructive, the first negative rebuttalist will need to pick and choose which arguments to carry though. Do not ignore arguments raised for the first time in the second affirmative constructive speech. Many judges consider the second negative rebuttal speech too late for a first response to second affirmative constructive speech arguments.

Strategy: To extend the negative's case attacks.

Duties:

1. Define terms. Decide if the affirmative has adequately defended its definition of terms. If it has, drop the argument. If not, explain why the affirmative definition of terms is still not acceptable.
2. If topicality was an issue in the first negative constructive, decide if the argument has been adequately answered. If the negative still feels that the affirmative case is not topical, refute the second affirmative constructive arguments and extend the negative explanation of why the case is not topical.
3. Return to the rest of the argumentation in the first negative speech, refuting the affirmative's objections. Keep in mind that time may not allow the first negative to return to every point. Carefully choose important points, develop these, and explain why they are the most important case arguments in the debate.
4. Look again at the affirmative's justification for change.
5. Give a summary of the negative block.

The conclusion of the first negative rebuttal should relate the negative's position on case (justification for change) to the plan objections just presented. A good structure here is an "even-if" development. It establishes that the need doesn't exist, but that, even if it did, the plan is significantly unable to meet it and/or creates disadvantages that lead to rejection of the plan. This conclusion of the first negative rebuttal makes a complete unit of the negative position.

QUESTIONS FOR DISCUSSION

1. The second negative constructive speech and the first negative rebuttal speech are known as the _____.

2. Why should the first negative rebuttalist not ignore the arguments presented by the second affirmative constructive speaker?

First Affirmative Rebuttal Speech

The *first affirmative rebuttal speech* is one of the most difficult speeches in the debate. The reason is that the first affirmative rebuttalist must respond to two negative speeches. This is a lot of ground to cover. This four- or five-minute speech (depending on which debate format is being used) is the affirmative's response to 12 or 15 minutes of uninterrupted negative argument. The difficulty of this speech can be eased with good use of organization and a concise use of language. The first affirmative rebuttalist must answer all new material presented by the second negative constructive speaker. In most cases, these arguments will deal with the affirmative plan. However, time must be kept in reserve to respond to the most important case arguments presented by the first negative rebuttal speaker.

Strategy: To further the affirmative's strategies of fulfilling the burden of proof, validating the affirmative plan, and narrowing the debate both on case and on plan.

Duties:
1. Refute the negative's plan objections. Try to consolidate as many arguments as possible. Point out fallacies (flaws) in reasoning, as well as missing links in arguments. When possible, try to show how negative disadvantages are really affirmative advantages.
2. Return to the affirmative's case to rebuild it at major points of attack. Choose arguments carefully. Attempt to narrow the debate by focusing the affirmative's argument on a few issues. Explain why these are the important issues.
3. Consolidate as many first negative rebuttal arguments as possible.
4. Give a brief summary that emphasizes the strengths of the affirmative's case.

Much ground must be covered and covered quickly enough to stay within the time limits but thoroughly enough for the responses to have an impact on the debate. In a five-minute rebuttal speech, it is often suggested that one spend three minutes on plan attacks and two minutes on case. In a four-minute rebuttal speech, it is suggested that two minutes to two and one-half minutes be spent on plan attacks and the balance on case. You will have to decide for yourself within any given round how to allocate your time effectively. Remember to watch the time carefully, allocate it wisely, and make every word count as you speak.

QUESTIONS FOR DISCUSSION

1. Why is the first affirmative rebuttal speech one of the most difficult speeches in the debate?

2. What should be the strategy for the first affirmative rebuttal speech?

3. In a five-minute rebuttal speech, what should be the time split between case and plan arguments?

4. How should the first affirmative rebuttalist narrow the debate?

Second Negative Rebuttal Speech

Since this is its last chance to speak in the debate, the negative must carefully choose which arguments to extend. First negative and second negative must work together to decide what the voting issues (reasons to vote either affirmative or negative) are. At the end of the second negative rebuttal, the negative wants the judge to view the arguments presented in this speech as the most important arguments in the round. Again, time is short, and there is much ground to cover. A good rule to follow is to spend two minutes on case arguments and three minutes on plan arguments (assuming the rebuttal is five minutes in length). Because plan arguments are still the newest arguments in the debate, they will take the most amount of time to cover and extend.

Strategy: To identify the case arguments the negative views as voting issues and to demonstrate that the significance of the disadvantages outweighs the advantages or the solvency of the affirmative harm.

Duties:

1. Give a brief introduction and a road map of the direction of the speech.
2. Briefly reestablish topicality and definition-of-terms challenges, if still applicable.
3. Reestablish key case arguments as voting issues and extend them for the negative.
4. Review plan objections and disadvantages, refuting the affirmative's responses and pointing to the issues the affirmative neglected to discuss. Again, time may not allow reviewing all the second negative arguments. Carefully choose the disadvantages that are most important to the negative. If necessary, drop the rest.
5. Summarize the negative position, calling for the rejection of the proposition.

Remember, the second negative rebuttalist is presenting the last word on all of the negative's positions (case and plan). Communication between first negative and second negative is imperative. First negative can probably identify voting issues on case better than the second negative can. At the same time, second negative is in a better position to identify the voting issues on the plan. Whether the second negative rebuttalist covers case or plan first is up to the individual. Some debaters make the decision depending on the individual round, ending each second negative rebuttal with the most important voting issues. In some rounds these issues are on case and in others they are on the plan. Other debaters go to case first and end with plan attacks because this is considered the negative offensive ground. If you think you have more arguments than available time, the second negative might decide to begin the rebuttal with the most important voting issues, rather than ending with them. Then, if something is dropped at the end, it will be the least rather than the most important issue. Negatives can win the round by winning any one of the important voting issues. The key is to think, communicate, and stay organized.

QUESTIONS FOR DISCUSSION

1. What does the term *voting issues* mean?

2. In a five-minute rebuttal speech, what is the recommended time split for plan and case arguments? Why?

3. What should be the strategy for the second negative rebuttal speech?

Second Affirmative Rebuttal Speech

The *second affirmative rebuttal speech* follows the last negative speech in debate. It is the conclusion of the arguments in the round. Like any other rebuttal, the second affirmative rebuttal should not contain new arguments. A new argument is a line of reasoning or emphasis raised for the first time in the debate.

Strategy: To put the debate in perspective, continue to advance the affirmative's basic strategies in the debate.

Duties:
1. Give a brief introduction and provide a road map of the speech.
2. Extend answers to plan objections. Take special care to refute major disadvantages and point out those that were dropped by the second negative rebuttalist. Continue to group negative arguments where possible.
3. Try to center the speech on the three or four major arguments on which the affirmative's case depends. If these are different from those identified by the negative, explain why.
4. Review the basic affirmative analysis and call for the acceptance of the proposition.

The second affirmative rebuttal speaker is in a unique position. He or she has the final opportunity to crystalize the debate for the judge. If arguments have become muddled or confused, this is the last chance to clarify them. It is the responsibility of the second affirmative rebuttal speaker to explain what the arguments mean in terms of the context of the debate round. For example, he or she might demonstrate why the advantages or solvency of the affirmative harm outweigh a disadvantage the negative may be winning. The speaker should be honest. He or she should not misrepresent what has or has not been said in the round.

QUESTIONS FOR DISCUSSION

1. Can the rebuttal speaker make new arguments in the rebuttal speech?

2. How should the second affirmative rebuttal speaker try to narrow the debate in this last speech of the debate?

4

An Examination
of Propositions

Generally, the topics selected for debate are similar to those being confronted in our "real world" problem solving arenas, such as the legislatures and courts of law. A good example of this parallel situation occurred in 1973 when the college debate topic concerned the availability of energy. Just as debaters were attending their first tournament of the year, the Organization of Petroleum Energy Countries (OPEC) moved to halt oil sales to the United States. Student debaters found themselves to be very well acquainted with the strengths and weaknesses of an important and current policy issue. Because debaters argue both sides of issues, it is necessary for them to analyze public policy. A result is that debaters are well-informed citizens. After reading this chapter, you should understand the following key terms:

problem area	proposition of policy
proposition of fact	proposition of value

In this chapter we will look at how propositions are formed and the types of propositions available for debate. Finally, we will see why the wording of a proposition is important and what role the audience plays in the debate.

THE PROBLEM AREA

A *problem area* is a general subject of concern to a community or group of people. Typically, problem areas are broad enough to encompass many particular questions. Water pollution is a problem area. Clean water, good farming practices, and pesticide use are specific issues that can be discussed within the area.

To narrow the problem area you begin by outlining the goals of the present system. Then you ask what is being done to reach these goals, has it been successful? After finding out where the present system has not been successful in reaching its goals you will use analysis to determine the causes of failure. You will find the following questions helpful in identifying possible propositions:

1. Is there a desirable goal within the problem area that has not been met?

2. How much progress has been made in reaching the goal?

3. Why hasn't the goal been reached? What are the obstacles?

4. What solutions could be implemented to overcome these obstacles?

5. Comparatively, which of the identified solutions would be most effective in reaching the goal?

By answering these five questions, you will be able to better determine the strengths and weaknesses of the problem area. It will also help you determine where research is needed as well as aid in laying out a plan of research. Finally, it will help you to pinpoint some of the issues you must consider in your own presentation of an opinion.

ACTIVITY   1. Select a problem area of interest to you. Using the questions above analyze the strengths and weaknesses of the problem area. Is it usable for debate?

PROPOSITIONS

A *resolution* is a proposition that is offered for consideration. It requires explanation, discussion, and proof. Trivial resolutions may go undisputed. Others may be worded so vaguely that no one wants to raise a disagreement. A proposition for debate should present a clear and important choice. There should be an important problem with definite possible solutions.

A proposition narrows the general discussion area. It provides a starting and ending point. Instead of examining all aspects of water pollution, for example, the proposition directs attention to a specific aspect of the water pollution problem that merits attention. It is also a means by which a solution to a problem can be found.

Choosing a Proposition   In high school debate, a national debate topic is chosen each year. The topic is debated for one academic year. First, the National University Extension Association's Committee on Discussion and Debate selects some topics. Then, the Committee mails ballots to all forensics teachers and even some students. After the preferences are tallied, the Committee verifies the balloting. High school topics for the past several years clearly show the variety and scope of issues that the selection process has resulted in:

Resolved: That governmental financial support for all public elementary and secondary education in the United States should be provided exclusively by the federal government.

Resolved: That the method of selecting presidential and vice-presidential candidates should be significantly changed.

Resolved: That a comprehensive program of penal reform should be adopted throughout the United States.

Resolved: That the federal government should guarantee comprehensive medical care for all citizens in the United States.

Resolved: That the federal government should establish a comprehensive program to significantly increase the energy independence of the United States.

Resolved: That the United States should significantly curtail its arms sales to other countries.

Resolved: That the federal government should provide employment for all employable United States citizens living in poverty.

Resolved: That the federal government should establish a comprehensive national policy to protect the quality of water in the United States.

Resolved: That the federal government should implement a comprehensive long-term agricultural policy in the United States.

On the college level, a different topic selection committee is responsible for putting together a ballot that is voted on each year by every debate program belonging to the National Debate Tournament. Many colleges debate a single topic for one academic year.

Once the resolution has been selected, the process of analysis focuses on that resolution. You will notice that each of the resolutions listed above deals with national or international affairs. All of these resolutions have a number of other characteristics in common. First, the propositions are worded so that the affirmative team (the side advocating the propositions) is on the side suggesting a change in the present system. The negative team, which argues against the proposition, is always placed in the position of defending the present system (that which already exists). Debaters are never asked to debate a question that would put the affirmative in the position of defending the present state of affairs. The topic "Resolved: That the United States should not significantly curtail its arms sales to other countries" would have to be changed to read "Resolved: That the United States should significantly curtail its arms sales to other countries."

Second, each of the topics advocates only *one* change in the present system. The affirmative is asked to advocate only one change of policy and the negative is asked to defend only one element of the present system. It might be interesting to debate "Resolved: That the Congress provide financial support for all public elementary and secondary schools and that the federal government should establish minimal educational standards for elementary and secondary schools in the United States." But such a topic should be subdivided into two separate propositions, and a decision made about which topic to use:

Resolved: That the Congress provide financial support for all public elementary and secondary schools.

Resolved: That the federal government should establish minimal educational standards for elementary and secondary schools in the United States.

The affirmative, however, is not limited to advocating a solution to a single harm. For example, under the education topic the affirmative might decide to present two problems—high dropout rates in high schools and the lack of adequate vocational educational programs. The solutions to these problems would be separate, but each would fall under the topic of elementary and secondary education.

Finally, the propositions are worded so as not to reflect a bias and so that the terms will be relatively clear to both the audience and the debaters. The topic (on page 34) that deals with a program of comprehensive medical care would have been improperly worded if its author had written "burdensome, incompetent comprehensive medical care." Also, the negative can be much more certain of the affirmative's interpretation of the topic if the wording contains a specific formulation, such as "comprehensive medical care."

Generally, then, a topic will fall within certain limits: (1) the affirmative team will always be placed in the position of advocating a change in the present system; (2) only one change in the present system will be suggested; and (3) the topic will be worded so as not to be biased.

QUESTIONS FOR DISCUSSION

1. Propositions are worded so that the affirmative is _____ the proposition.

2. Is the affirmative ever asked to defend the present system?

3. How many ideas are there in a proposition?

ACTIVITY

1. None of the propositions listed below falls within the limits outlined for propositions. Why?

Resolved: That schools should establish criteria for exemption from final exams and require minimum competency tests for graduation.

Resolved: That the military draft is not necessary to ensure national security.

Resolved: That a judge is better qualified to render a verdict than is a jury of common, everyday citizens.

Resolved: That the federal government should provide a guaranteed annual income and medical care for all United States citizens.

Resolved: That the federal government should guarantee employment for all unskilled and uneducated persons seeking a job.

Resolved: That schools should not be responsible for the future employability of their graduating students.

TYPES OF PROPOSITIONS

Propositions are of three types—propositions of *fact,* propositions of *value,* and propositions of *policy.* Each requires its own unique kind of support, explanation, development, and proof.

Propositions of Fact

A *proposition of fact* is an objective statement that something exists. It asserts that a condition exists that can be verified by someone other than the person making the statement. A proposition of fact may be about some object or event that can be experienced directly by the physical senses of sight, hearing, touch, smell, and taste. "Carrots are an orange and nutritious vegetable" is a factual statement about a tangible object. It can be verified through the senses by someone other than the person making the statement. "Vegetables are nutritious" is a more general statement. However, it is still a proposition of fact because the truth of the statement can be determined scientifically.

Generally, propositions of fact are considered the simplest and least controversial of the three types of propositions. That does not mean they are uncontroversial. There can be disagreements over propositions of fact. For example, every criminal court trial involves at least one controversial proposition of fact. The prosecution contends that the accused committed a crime; the defense disagrees. And during the trial the prosecution's proposition of fact is debated. Propositions of fact are less controversial than propositions of value or policy because they can usually be verified objectively by reference to other facts. As in a court of law the commitment of an action can be determined by looking at the facts relevant to the case.

Statements of fact may be about the past, as well as the present. A newspaper report or a story from history can qualify as factual propositions. A statement of fact may be asserted by someone other than an actual witness. The statement, however, still must be objective and verifiable. Verifying a fact (its existence or nonexistence) does not hinge on the credibility or experience of the person making the assertion. All that is necessary is an independent method of verification.

While propositions of fact are not used in competitive debate, they can be of value in an academic setting—for example, in social studies, English, philosophy, political science, civics, and economics classes. Clubs and organizations may also consider them more frequently than other types of propositions. Generally, they will choose an area of interest or concern to their members or to the community as a whole. Propositions of fact tend to be narrower in scope than propositions of value or policy. And they can work quite well in debates conducted before general audiences.

The issues inherent in propositions of fact are relatively few. The student needs to determine (1) what occurred, (2) what information is required to verify the occurrence, and (3) what information is available for use. Consideration of these issues will result in accurate analysis of propositions of fact. Listed below are some examples of propositions of fact.

Resolved: That television viewing contributes to the increasing crime rate.

Resolved: That more than half of America's children are presently growing up in single-parent homes.

Resolved: That vocational education programs in high schools reduce the dropout rate.

Resolved: That children attending preschool are better prepared socially for kindergarten.

Resolved: That exemption-from-final-exam options increase student grade averages.

Resolved: That federal intervention in church schools is unconstitutional.

QUESTIONS FOR DISCUSSION

1. What is a *proposition of fact*?

2. What does time have to do with propositions of fact?

3. What are the issues surrounding propositions of fact?

ACTIVITY

1. The following propositions have been identified as propositions of fact. Some are indeed propositions of fact, while others are not. Find those propositions which are not propositions of fact. Rewrite each one so that it is a proposition of fact.

Resolved: That the federal deficit should be eliminated.

Resolved: That the federal government should establish a comprehensive energy policy to achieve energy independence in the United States.

Resolved: That a college degree makes an individual more employable than a high school degree does.

Resolved: That fresh vegetable prices fluctuate with the growing seasons.

Resolved: That children with two years of preschool are better prepared for kindergarten than are those without preschool.

Propositions of Value

Propositions of value express judgment about the qualities of a person, place, thing, idea, or event. A statement of value concerns opinions and attitudes. When you say, "More than half of America's children are presently growing up in single-parent homes," you are making a factual statement. But when you say, "Children living in single-parent homes are less well off than other children," you are giving an opinion about the quality of the home environment; you are making a value judgment.

Knowing the facts about a given situation is enlightening, but it is values that determine how people respond to a situation. As we said earlier, facts are either true or false. They can be verified. But values are neither true nor false. At best it can be verified that you hold a particular value, but it cannot be verified that you should or should not hold the value. To say that football is boring is to say something about your attitude towards football, not about football itself. To someone else, football might be the most exciting sport. Although values are not verifiable, they are important because we hold them, and we allow them to color our thinking about everything else.

Propositions of value are statements of judgment. They concern a thing's qualities, rather than the thing itself. Judgments are important because they express opinions and attitudes about facts and events—whether we like them or dislike them, whether they are good or bad, whether they should lead to action, and, if so, what type of action they should lead to. The following are some examples of propositions of value:

Resolved: That the United States' defense budget is adequate to ensure national security.

Resolved: That three years of English in high school is adequate for a basic education.

Resolved: That modern art is lacking in artistic skill and creativity.

Resolved: That volunteer work strengthens the character of the individual.

Resolved: That adequate medical care is a right, not a privilege.

When you decide that a problem is significant or harmful, you are making a value judgment. To say that a plan has results that could be called advantageous or disadvantageous is to make a value judgment. Ultimately, to recommend action on a policy change and to specify the types of government actions that should or should not be adopted is to make value judgments. Every persuasive appeal in debate inevitably calls forth the values held by those listening to you. Your success in a debate round will be enhanced by your understanding of the nature of values, how they function as guides to creating arguments, and how your listeners will use their own values when they evaluate your speech.

While there are many important values, there is no established priority of values. When relevant values conflict, priority must be determined. A good example of competing values was shown recently in the public controversy over mandatory air bags for automobiles. Though few people questioned the fact that air bags installed in all cars could save thousands of lives, the government decided not to require auto manufacturers to install them because it seemed that the public would rather have the choice to buy air bags as a voluntary option. In this instance, the value of free choice was held to be more important than the value of life. A counter example is that of seat belts. In the last couple of years, many states have begun to require that everyone in the front seat must be wearing a seat belt. In this case it was decided that the value of life was more important than the value of free choice.

Many people enjoy debating propositions of value. Anyone who listens to television talk shows is bound to hear debates about value judgments. They create audience interest because people react personally to such judgments as "the Cubs are a good team" or "rock videos should have moral ratings." Even though it is impossible to validate value judgements, the purpose of debates based on propositions of value is to create interest and to clarify points of view, not to arrive at conclusions.

QUESTIONS FOR DISCUSSION

1. What is a *proposition of value*?

2. Can you verify the truth or falsity of a proposition of value? Why or why not?

3. Propositions of value are statements of _____.

ACTIVITY

1. The following resolutions have been identified as propositions of value. However, not all of them meet the criteria of a value proposition. Identify those that are not propositions of value and rewrite them as propositions of value. If you feel that a proposition cannot be made into a proposition of value, explain why.

Resolved: That two years of math is essential to a well-rounded education.

Resolved: That President Kennedy was killed by a lone assassin.

Resolved: That all U.S. citizens desiring work should be guaranteed a job.

Resolved: That each school should designate a smoking area on school grounds for students.

Resolved: That all Americans are entitled to a home and minimal nutrition.

Propositions of Policy

A *proposition of policy* is a statement of a course of action to be considered for adoption. If adopted it is intended to guide present and future government and/or private sector decisions. In a corporation, for example, company policies govern employer-employee relations. A school district may set up policies governing how the school buildings may be used by outside groups. Local, state, and federal legislators pass policies that administrative branches of government are expected to enforce.

As we noted earlier, a proposition is a statement for consideration. A proposition of policy calls for an action or decision. It differs from the proposition of fact or value in that it is not subject to verification by observation of events or objects, nor is it validated by agreement among all the people subject to the policy and imposed on them by force of law. Because policies are created and maintained ultimately by the agreement of the people they affect, they are considered to be subject to change through orderly processes. Policies are generally considered negotiable. Broadly speaking, any statement of a policy is a proposition of policy. However, in debate we usually focus our attention on propositions of policy requiring consideration, that is, propositions for which we seek to gain acceptance. There are three general categories of propositions of policy.

First, you may propose a new policy to guide decisions and actions where no policy exists. This is the starting point for all policies. Recall our earlier example of the dress code. In the 1950s and early 1960s, students dressed rather formally. During the sixties came the mini-skirt and long hair for boys (known to some as the hippy look). Administrators could not arbitrarily decide which students were not dressed properly for school and send them home. In an effort to bring order to the situation, the administration and the student body (and, in some cases, parents) worked together to develop a dress code for schools. The administration sent students home when they were found to be in violation of the code. A whole new set of policies was put into place where none had previously existed.

Second, you may propose amendments to alter policies that exist but for some reason are no longer satisfactory. The conditions that existed originally may have changed in significant ways, making established policies outmoded. A good example of an amended policy is the reduction of the speed limit on interstate highways from 70 miles per hour (in some cases, 75) to 55 miles per hour, in order to reduce the nation's fuel consumption during the 1973 oil crisis. As the fuel crisis has eased, some states have begun to consider changing this policy once again. The future may see speed limits increasing again to 70 miles per hour.

Third, you may propose to abolish an existing policy altogether. Once it was an education requirement for all high school students to study Latin. Now, only a few college graduate programs maintain such a policy. At some point, the educational authorities decided to abandon the policy of requiring the study of languages other than English. Industry used to be able to force workers to retire at age 65. Now (with a few exceptions), an employee can stay on the job as long as he or she is capable of performing the work required. Industry has been forced to replace a policy of mandatory retirement with a program of enticements for retirement and early retirement.

During the round each team puts forth its arguments for or against the proposition to an impartial judge, who is responsible for making a final decision to accept or reject the proposition based on the merits of the case as presented in the individual debate round. The debaters are not expected to reach a conclusion in the round but only to present their case to the judge. The following are some examples of propositions of policy:

Resolved: That the United States should provide a guaranteed annual income for all citizens.

Resolved: That the federal government should establish national standards for the certification of elementary and secondary school teachers.

Resolved: That the federal government should initiate and enforce safety guarantees on consumer goods.

Resolved: That the jury system should be abolished.

Resolved: That the United States should adopt a comprehensive program of energy conservation.

Resolved: That the federal government should implement programs to curtail rising unemployment.

Resolved: That the federal government should establish a comprehensive national policy to protect the quality of air in the United States.

Each of these propositions proposes a rule, regulation, or law to govern decisions within a designated problem area. Although the statements are general, they state an agency of jurisdiction ("the federal government" or "the United States") and an action in a specific direction ("implement programs" or "establish a comprehensive policy").

QUESTIONS FOR DISCUSSION

1. What is a *proposition of policy*?

2. How does a proposition of policy differ from a proposition of fact or value?

3. What are the three general categories of propositions of policy? Define each.

ACTIVITIES

1. The following propositions have been identified as propositions of policy. Identify those propositions which are not propositions of policy. Rewrite them as propositions of policy.

Resolved: That the federal government should establish guidelines to guarantee safety in the NASA space program.

Resolved: That zoning ordinances in Los Angeles should not be significantly changed.

Resolved: That the lack of an adequate diet is harmful to one's health.

Resolved: That increases in military spending are detrimental to social programs.

Resolved: That the federal government should establish a computer network for identifying and locating missing children.

2. Following are three propositions. Choose one and answer the questions listed below.

Resolved: That the federal government should establish a mandatory seat belt law.

Resolved: That the federal government should reinstitute the military draft.

Resolved: That the federal government should establish a program to provide for aging American citizens.

    a. Is the proposition debatable? Why or why not?
    b. Is the proposition controversial? Why or why not?
    c. Is this a significant problem? Why or why not?
    d. Generally, what is the history of this problem?
    e. Are there any laws, regulations, or rules, pertaining to this problem? Do they need to be strengthened? Are they inappropriate? Are they adequate? Why or why not?
    f. What kinds of solutions might be considered for this problem?
    g. What basic areas might you explore for the affirmative?

THE WORDING OF A PROPOSITION

For purposes of analysis, it is necessary to define each term of the debate proposition. Let us examine the 1986–87 high school debate resolution: "Resolved: That the federal government should implement a comprehensive long-term agricultural policy in the United States." Analysis begins by identifying the terms of importance and defining each word. In this proposition, key terms are

Federal Government—identifies who should instigate change
Implement—identifies the direction of policy implementation
Comprehensive—qualifies the nature of the policy
Long-Term—qualifies the nature of the policy
Agriculture—the action desired by the proposition
Policy—the action desired by the proposition

A well-worded resolution clearly identifies who should act and what ought to be done. Sometimes words are ambiguous. There are several sources available that will assist you in defining terms. First, you may consult dictionaries, textbooks, and encyclopedias, which will give you an idea of general usage. You may also check the definitions of terms in specialized sources, which will be helpful with technical terms. Publications such as *Black's Law Dictionary* and *The American Dictionary of Psychology,* for example, may be consulted if the topic falls into the legal or social areas. Also, consider how the terms are used within social, political, economic, and historical texts. As you begin your research, you will want to note carefully how the terms are used by the experts in the field.

Almost all resolutions contain words that are labeled *value* terms. In the farm policy resolution, the value term is "comprehensive." Other value terms that might appear in a resolution are *fair, new, significant, best, control, exclusively, guarantee,* and *benefit*. These are value terms because they are subject to interpretation. Their meanings are indefinite or imprecise. Before agreement can be reached on a solution to a problem, everyone must agree on the terms being used. When debating the resolution "Resolved: That the United States should significantly change its foreign trade policies," you must fully understand what a *significant* change is.

QUESTIONS FOR DISCUSSION

1. Your analysis of any proposition should begin by _____ each term of the resolution.

2. While the first place to look for a definition of a term is the dictionary, where else would you want to look for how a term is used?

3. What is a *value term*?

ACTIVITIES

1. Two specialized dictionaries were listed above. Look in the library for other specialized dictionaries or publications that could be used to define terms. Make a list of them.

2. Using the resolution below, identify and define the terms of the resolution. Be sure to check specialized dictionaries, as well as general use dictionaries.

Resolved: That the United States should adopt a comprehensive program of energy conservation.

THE AUDIENCE

The next area to be considered is the intended *audience*. What you say and do with the information you accumulate on a topic will be influenced to some extent by the audience to which you are speaking. You will need to determine which issues will best speak to the particular interests of the audience you are addressing. Let's look at an example on the agriculture topic presented earlier. If your audience is a group of farmers, you would not want to argue directly that farm bankruptcies are not significantly harmful. Nor would you want to argue that "the free ride" is over. Price supports should be eliminated. Your audience is not likely to be receptive to such arguments.

Audience analysis helps you to select arguments that will win group support for your position. You should survey your list of possible arguments, consider your audience, and then decide which arguments to make and how to make them. For example, if you must defend the proposition that farm bankruptcies are not significantly harmful, you will have to *lead* your audience of farmers to that conclusion. How can you do this? First, provide statistics on the number of bankruptcies versus the number of farmers. Second, compare these figures to those of other businesses. Third, outline programs (federal, state, and local) which are available to help farmers. Fourth, illustrate what happens to a farmer after a bankruptcy.

The farmers may not like what they are hearing, but this approach makes it more difficult for them to tune you out. In academic debate, the aim of an advocate is to show that a policy will result in the greatest good for the greatest number of people. There is no requirement to show that the policy benefits any special group.

Still, every debate requires audience adaptation. In addition to accurate analysis of a problem area, you must communicate information in a clear, concise manner. Arguments must be interesting and well chosen. A debater is first and foremost an advocate who must persuade.

QUESTION FOR DISCUSSION

1. Why is it important to analyze your audience when you are deciding what arguments to use and how to present them?

ACTIVITY

1. Using the resolution below, identify five audiences that might be very biased for or against the resolution. Explain why.

Resolved: That the United States should significantly change its foreign trade policies.

5

Developing
Research Skills

Preparing for a debate might be compared to preparing for an exam. The exam itself may take only an hour to complete but studying for the exam will have taken place over several days or weeks. Why is so much time needed to prepare to debate? The answer is *research*. One must do research to gather evidence to support the arguments used in a debate. In *competitive* debate it is not unusual for a debater to spend days searching for a specific piece of evidence to support a single argument. It is quite likely that the argument itself will only take 30 seconds to deliver in the actual debate! When beginning your research you need to understand the following key terms:

brief	indexes (or guides)
card catalog	key terms
evidence	research
evidence card	

The debater wants to gather information to support potential arguments. When put into a usable form, this information is referred to as *evidence*. An argument is the process of reasoning from the known to the unknown—from *evidence* to a *conclusion*. An argument, then, needs evidence for an audience to accept it as valid. Because each debate contains many arguments and the debater participates in more than one debate, he or she needs a significant amount of evidence to deal intelligently with a single topic. With the gathering of evidence should come a thorough understanding of the issues in the topic area. Without such an understanding, the debater will find it difficult to apply the evidence he or she has gathered. In national collegiate debate the most successful debaters tend to be those with a thorough understanding of the topic and the best evidence to support what they assert.

SEARCHING FOR EVIDENCE

The goal of research should be to obtain the highest-quality evidence possible. The quantity of evidence should never become more important than the quality of the evidence. One good, on-point piece of evidence will do more to support an argument than ten general pieces of evidence. To be able to obtain high-quality evidence, one must implement a plan of research. Reading books at random or haphazardly moving from one area of the topic to another will produce evidence, but usually not enough quality evidence to support a single argument. The debater must put into action a plan of research.

Blueprint Plan of Research   The best place to begin is at the beginning. The first step is brainstorming. *Brainstorming* is the process of searching one's own mind for ideas that might be relevant to the proposition. This can be done on an individual basis or in a group. Usually, the larger the number of people involved, the larger the number of ideas that will be generated. Make a list of all your ideas. This will be helpful when you move on to the next step, a library survey. The guide to what is available in the library is the *card catalog,* which lists all the books in the library by author, title, and subject. At this point you will be looking for books by subject. For example, if you are researching the 1986–87 high school debate topic, "Resolved: That the federal government should implement a comprehensive long-term agricultural policy in the United States," the first subject you will look up in the card catalog is *agriculture.* Next, you will refer to such specific aspects of agriculture as grain, crops, food, farms, wheat, and corn. While exploring your own list of areas, you will find additional areas cross-referenced in the card catalog. As you discover new areas be sure to keep a list of key terms. Do not trust your memory. Once you have completed a preliminary bibliography (list) of books from the card catalog, you will want to explore other general reference sources. Keep in mind that you will want to come back to the card catalog to update your bibliography as you discover new areas of the topic.

Reference books   For general information on your topic, you may find the following reference books useful:

- encyclopedias
- almanacs

- yearbooks
- reference guides (Winchell's *Guide to Reference Books* and Shore's *Basic Reference Books*)

While these sources may not produce evidence on the topic, they will give you background information. And this information will help you to go on to more technical sources later on. In addition, consult such *guides* and *indexes* as *The Reader's Guide to Periodical Literature* and *The International Index*. In these you will find alphabetical listings by author, title, and general subject of magazine articles that have appeared in a particular group of periodicals.

Indexes   On any topic to be debated, you may want to consult one or more of the various special indexes that are available. Most libraries carry the indexes listed below, although they may not carry all of the publications listed in them. Be sure to keep a list of promising articles listed in these indexes, even if your library does not carry the publication. You may have the opportunity at a later date to work in other libraries.

Bibliographical Index. A bibliography of bibliographies.
Education Index. A listing of articles and publications related to education.
Resources in Education
Current Index to Journals in Education
Books in Print. An annual listing of published works by subject, author, and title.
Forthcoming Books. A bimonthly listing of all books scheduled for publication within the next five months.
International Index to Periodicals. Alphabetical listings of magazine articles by author, title, and general subject.
Economic Index
Catholic Periodicals Index
Social Sciences and Humanities Index
The Bulletin of the Public Affairs Information Service
Public Affairs Information Service
Book Review Digest. An excellent place to find critical reviews of major sources.
Book Review Index. An excellent source of references to critical reviews.
Cumulative Book Index
United States Government Printing Office: Monthly Publications Catalog. A reference catalog listing all government publications by subject headings.
United States Government Printing Office: Congressional Information Service Index. Contains annotated listings of all publications from the legislative branch since 1970.
United Nations Document Index. Very useful, but frequently overlooked.
Index to Legal Periodicals
Foreign Affairs Bibliography
Biography Index
Current Biography
Who's Who in America. A standard source for substantiating the qualifications of authors. There are also several specialized *Who's Who* books.
The Congressional Quarterly of the Bulletin of the Public Affairs Information Service
Vertical File Index. Listing of a collection of clippings from assorted current periodicals and newspapers related to topics of current interest.

When you begin your research, keep in mind that each index and bibliography will be organized under many different broad subject headings. By all means use your imagination when you use an index. And make sure that your list of key terms is as comprehensive as possible. It is your list of key terms that will open the door to articles and books to research. Let's take the resolution "Resolved: That the federal government should provide employment for all employable United States citizens living in poverty." What are the obvious key terms which come to mind?

poverty	guaranteed annual income
public welfare	job training
public assistance	day care
unemployment compensation	standard of living

Now let's look at this topic again. With the obvious key terms behind us, what other areas or ideas might we consider when dealing with the topic of poverty?

health care	medicaid
social policy	hunger
social work	inflation
crime	productivity
retirement	technology
housing	protectionism
vocational education	immigration
riots	stress
medicare	military spending

Each of these terms may relate to the subject of poverty. For example, those who are unwillingly unemployed may be unhappy and restless and therefore provoked to *riot.* Also, advances in *technology* affect the number and type of jobs available. The federal government's position on illegal and legal *immigration* particularly affects the number of low-skilled jobs available to U.S. citizens. Remember, use your imagination. Think beyond the obvious.

QUESTIONS FOR DISCUSSION

1. What is a *card catalog*?

2. What are four types of reference books you might consult for background material?

3. What does *brainstorm* mean?

ACTIVITIES

1. Using the propositions provided below, make a list of key terms. Remember, use your imagination. Do not list just the obvious key terms.

   Resolved: That the federal government should take action to balance the budget of the federal government.

   Resolved: That the federal government should establish a comprehensive national policy to protect the quality of the air and water.

   Resolved: That students should be allowed a greater voice in the development of school policy.

   Resolved: That academic achievement criteria should be applied to extra-curricular activities for participation.

2. Using one of the resolutions in Activity 1, perform the following tasks:
   a. Make a list of books of interest on the proposition.
   b. Using one of the special indexes, make a bibliography of magazines (or books) available on the proposition.

HIGH QUALITY EVIDENCE

Deciding which kind of evidence is best is not easy. Because evidence is used to try to obtain agreement from an audience or a judge, the basic question is this: What does it take to get the listener to decide that the argument is valid? No doubt, some people require very little in the way of evidence to support what they already feel to be true. But even the best evidence might not cause people whose opinions have already been formed to change their minds. Some audiences require extremely sound evidence, while others seem to believe anything that has appeared in print.

In examining the criteria for debate evidence, it is best to look first at the general standards. The critic who listens to a debate and the debater who searches for evidence start by considering two general questions: (1) What can be said about the *external* qualities of the evidence—is the *source* of the evidence reliable? (2) What can be said about the *internal* qualities of the evidence—is it *truthful?*

External Criticism   Questions of external criticism (how good is the source?) can be divided into two areas: (1) the excellence of the publication from which the material is drawn and (2) the competence of the author of the material. Several criteria should be used in judging the quality of the publication and the qualifications of the author.

How good is the publication?   The publication should be respected, unbiased and qualified in the field being researched. If a magazine, for instance, claims to report current events, does it report these events reliably, or does it interpret events to fit a particular editorial bias?

What is the *form* of the evidence?   This question is quite complex. For example, two debate teams may differ as to what was or was not said in a presidential address, only to find that one team has been quoting from a source that utilized an advance copy of the speech, while the other team has been quoting from a source that used the speech as it was actually given. Another team may find that an authority has said something in a television discussion that is different from what he or she wrote in a scholarly book.

The general rule on the form of a source is that the more permanent the form, the more reliable the information. Authorities are likely to be more careful in a scholarly book that will be available for many years than in a television encounter that is only transitory. The President is likely to weigh every word carefully in the prepared text of a speech, simply because every word will be carefully read. He may feel freer to exaggerate and dramatize in off-the-cuff remarks. The debater, therefore, will seek the most permanent forms of evidence, because they typically represent the best material.

How competent is the author?   The first question to ask here is *who is the author?* The author should be professionally qualified and competent to state facts or opinions, should be respected by other authorities in the field, and should have a reputation for responsible reporting. An author should not be biased. The authority with a vested interest should be avoided. One would expect, for instance, that a physicist who is paid to test nuclear weapons would say that such testing is necessary. Thus, when you are researching a given authority, look for evidence that supports opinions other than that authority's. Evidence by a physicist stating that nuclear weapons did *not* need to be tested would be very valuable evidence.

A very common pitfall is that authorities in one field may state opinions about other fields in which they are not qualified. An expert in military strategy might express opinions about foreign policy. A physicist might offer medical advice to a friend. However, being a layperson does not make one's opinion false, any more than being an expert necessarily makes it true. The good debater is careful to gauge accurately the qualifications of the author of the evidence.

***When* did the author get the information?**

Generally, the closer the author was to the event, the more likely it is that the information will be right. In current events this usually means that the most recent evidence is the best. On many issues or arguments, the date of the evidence could determine who wins. For instance, a magazine article on a specific international proposal could become outdated with tomorrow's headlines. A poll of public opinion on a given subject might be out of date as soon as a new poll is published. In historical events it may well be that the oldest source is the most accurate. An ancient Greek's comments about life in ancient Greece may be more accurate than those in a modern, idealized version of that country.

Books are not printed with the same speed as magazines or newspapers. A book with a copyright date of 1986 was probably written in 1984 or 1985, at best. A good way to judge the timeliness of a book is to check the footnotes. The dates in the footnotes and in the bibliography will give you a good idea of when the book was actually written.

Internal Criticism

Internal criticism, concerned with the truth of the evidence, frequently is overlooked by inexperienced researchers. They feel that if the source is sound and the authority reputable, the evidence must be true. The U2 incident is a good example of the kind of exception that can occur. One can easily find quotations from the President of the United States, and in the best sources, that the U2 was a lost weather plane that had strayed over Russia. Later, the President was forced to admit that the plane was on a spying mission, deliberately flying over the Soviet Union. One should always read with caution.

What does it say?

In evaluating the validity of evidence, your first and most obvious question is *what does the evidence say*? What does it report, and does this report make sense?

Does the evidence report actual events—*facts*—or does it make *inferences* about what is probably true, based on what is already known? Or perhaps the statement is a *value judgment,* based on inferences drawn from facts. Most logicians feel that the further the statement is from the fact level, the more likely it is to contain an error. For example:

Fact level: This Olds Cutlass is a lemon.
Inference level: All Olds Cutlasses are lemons.
Value level: Do not buy an Olds Cutlass.

Many inexperienced debaters depend on opinion evidence in which bias and error are most likely to become significant. It is best to present evidence that is factual in nature and let the judge follow the debater's logic in arriving at his or her conclusions.

How consistent is it?

The truth of evidence can also be judged by checking to see if it is *consistent within itself.* It is not unusual to discover inconsistencies in evidence, and a careful researcher often can disprove the opponent's arguments by showing that the opposing team didn't read enough of the quotation to indicate the true opinion of the authority. Or one can read further in the same article or in other articles by the same person to show that the so-called authority seems unable to make up his or her mind. Inconsistency, then, may be one of the first indications that a piece of supporting material is not valid.

Do authorities agree? Finally, the validity of evidence can be gauged by determining whether it is *consistent with other information.* Do other authorities or sources agree? Is the same fact consistently observed by others? The researcher should beware of arguments for which only one supporting source can be found. One also should be careful of a quotation that runs counter to the bulk of other information.

QUESTIONS FOR DISCUSSION

1. In research you should consider two general questions before you record a piece of evidence. What are they?

2. Why is the quality of the source (publication) important?

3. Define a qualified author. Why is it important to know the qualifications of the author?

4. Why is the date on a piece of evidence important?

5. When you are examining the truth of a piece of evidence (internal criticism), what questions should you ask?

6. What is the difference between a fact, an inference, and a value?

ACTIVITIES

1. For one week watch the television news and read newspapers and magazines concerning a particular event. What differences did you see in the reporting of facts? Which source of information was better? Why? Make a collection of the articles.

2. Using the event you chose above, show how a date of the evidence could be an important factor if the information were used in a debate.

3. Bring to class the newspaper and magazine articles you collected for Activity 1. In class, mark quotations that could be used as evidence for *or* against the proposition. Also, answer these questions:
   a. Does each article have an author? If yes, do you know the qualifications of the author? If not, find them.
   b. Do you have the article titles and the newspaper or periodical titles?
   c. Do you have the date of publication for each source?
   d. Do you have the page numbers of the source?
   e. Is the source unbiased?
   f. Is the source reliable and respected by others?
      Be prepared to explain why you chose the articles.

RECORDING EVIDENCE

Thus far we have talked about what evidence is and how to find it. Now the question is, what do you do with it? First, you must decide exactly what portion of the article or book you should use to support your argument. Second, the portion (quotation) needs to be recorded so that it is usable (both in length and form). Finally, it should be recorded in such a way that you are able to answer questions about its accuracy. The end product is referred to as an *evidence card.*

Preparing Evidence Cards

The first step in developing an evidence card is isolating or marking the material to be copied. When you are copying material, be sure that the isolated material accurately reflects the intent of the author. The information should then be placed on a file card in such a way that it will be easy for you to use. It is recommended that the information be typed on a four-by-six-inch index card. This makes it easier for both colleagues to read the information, but it can also be written out in longhand.

The card should be clearly labeled with the citation of the source. The full bibliographical reference should be typed in block style on the card. For the judge's and opponent's benefits and for later reference, it is especially important that the source and page number be accurately noted. A good quotation can lose its impact if the opposition points out that it cannot find the quotation on the page that the debater reported. The author's qualifications should also be included on the card, and space should be left in one corner for a filing index code.

Only one piece of evidence should be put on an index card. It will cause a great deal of confusion later if there are two quotations on one index card. It will be hard to find your evidence and hard to file it. Here are two typical evidence card entries:

> Albert Karr (staff reporter), "Reagan Plans to Urge Smaller Cutback in U.S. Support to Agricultural Service," *Wall Street Journal*, January 23, 1986, p. 6.
>
> "The law [Gramm-Rudmann] could require an across-the-board cut in the total federal budget of $50 billion to $60 billion if Congress fails to reduce the projected fiscal 1987 deficit to $144 billion by October 1, the start of the fiscal year."

> Pat M. Holt (former chief of staff of the Senate Foreign Relations Committee), "Beyond Today's African Hunger: Population Pressure," *The Christian Science Monitor*, February 5, 1986, p. 17.
>
> "Rains in Africa last year have provided a breathing space in which we can think about the long-term agricultural policies of that continent."

It is not wise to delete words when recording a piece of evidence. However, if unnecessary words are ommitted, the omission should be clearly indicated with ellipses (...). Adjectives, qualifiers, and such words as "not" are not considered unnecessary words. It is strongly suggested that ellipses be avoided whenever possible. What you consider unnecessary may be considered essential to someone else. The National Forensics League now requires that internal ellipses not be used unless the team has in its possession the original or a copy of the original. Always check to be sure that each piece of evidence can stand on its own. Any references to "it," "he," "the act," or "the program" should indicate what is being referred to. Note the qualification in the following piece of evidence:

"He [Ruckelshaus] emphasized again that Congress, in its current consideration of Superfund, could add such responsibilities that would do more harm than help."

Notice that without the word "Ruckelshaus," the quotation would be incomplete. You cannot rely on your memory to recall the person the "he" refers to. Remember, you will be recording many more than one piece of evidence. While ellipses should be avoided, it is helpful to put [brackets] around words in the quotation that need not be read. Such material sometimes makes the quotation confusing or unnecessarily long and is best deleted. This way the entire quotation is still available for anyone who wants to check the original.

Many students find that word processors are a real help when they are recording evidence and prefer to record such evidence on *briefs* rather than on research cards. A brief is the development of an idea or argument in outline form. The evidence or logical reasoning is provided for each subpoint. Briefs can be made for both affirmative and negative arguments.

Each brief should be limited to the development of only one argument. The word processor makes it easy for the debater to take evidence from several sources and rewrite it into one compelling brief.

QUESTIONS FOR DISCUSSION

1. When you are putting a quotation on an evidence card, what information about the quotation do you need to include?

2. Why is it unwise to use ellipses on evidence cards?

ACTIVITIES

1. Using the articles you marked for quotations, make evidence cards. Be sure to check your evidence for accuracy and references ("it" or "he"). When you are finished, compare your evidence to the examples on page 51.

FILING EVIDENCE

There will come a point in time when you will have accumulated a significant number of evidence cards. As you accumulate more and more evidence, it becomes very important for you to be able to retrieve it for use in a debate round. If you cannot find your evidence when you need it, it loses its value. Information retrieval, then, is as important as your original research.

Usually, each student develops a filing system that works best for him or her. Any system is adequate if the students know at all times what they have and can quickly retrieve the evidence during a debate. The important thing, again, is not so much what system you use but that you use a system. There are, however, several commonly used filing systems that vary in complexity, depending on how much evidence the researcher has gathered.

The common feature of all the systems is that the student divides the evidence into categories. Then, the material is stored in a file box behind index cards that indicate the category. No matter what system is used, it is important that the number of cards in each category be kept small. If there are more than *ten* cards under a single heading, the chances increase that you won't know what the file contains and will use the first card you find. Even if you know what evidence is in the file, a category that contains a great many cards will take too long to sort through in an actual debate round. A filing system should make it as easy as possible to find evidence during a round.

Alphabetical Filing System

The most elementary filing system involves dividing the cards into subject areas and arranging the subjects alphabetically. If the researcher has several cards on agricultural exports, they are filed behind an index card (divider card) labeled "Agricultural Exports" in the upper right-hand corner of each card to facilitate refiling. This system is used most often by new debaters, and it works fairly well as long as you have a small number of evidence cards. Most evidence, however, requires a more elaborate system.

As debaters get more and more evidence, it becomes necessary to develop a more elaborate system. What is needed is two file boxes, one for the affirmative and one for the negative evidence. The cards are then filed behind the major affirmative and negative headings.

Such a system, unfortunately, presents problems. To begin with, it takes a great deal of time during a debate to find the appropriate heading and then to find the best card. Also, a sizable amount of material cannot easily be classified as either affirmative or negative. For these reasons, a notebook index system may prove more useful.

Notebook Index System

In a notebook index system the index file cards (divider cards) are numbered instead of labeled by subject. "Agricultural Exports" might become "Category A." Cards that deal with Soviet exports might be numbered "A14." A master notebook is then kept for the entire filing system. All of the material in each file box is noted on a single index sheet to which one can quickly refer for code numbers that apply to specific subjects. The number of cards in each category is kept small by expanding the number of categories and by eliminating the weakest evidence.

Each file box should be assigned a code number. Each major heading should receive a letter and each subcategory a number. The index sheet provides the summary for the filed material. The following is part of an index sheet that might be used on a water pollution topic.

Sample Index System

A. Role of States in the Environmental Process
    1. Clean Water Act prompts state action
    2. State enforcement variations result in pollution shopping
    3. State cannot afford water quality costs
    4.
    5.
    6.
    7.
    8.
    9.
  10.
  11. State programs are good
  12. State programs are supported by the people
  13. States have effective enforcement
  14. States have adequate jurisdictional authority
  15. States can afford to spend more on toxic cleanup
  16.
  17.
  18.
  19.
  20.
  21.
  22.

B. Environmental Protection Agency
   1. *Milwaukee v. Illinois* prevents common law remedies
   2. Personnel shortage
   3. EPA lowered standards for cancer-causing chemicals
   4. Enforcement is necessary
   5. EPA favors degrading water quality
   6. EPA not careful in regulating toxics
   7. EPA enforcement is decentralized and uncoordinated
   8. EPA does not have recourse to criminal sanctions
   9.
   10.
   11.
   12.
   13.
   14.
   15.
   16. EPA intent on promulgating effective guidelines
   17. *Exxon* case gives EPA less discretion
   18. Lack of EPA enforcement encourages environmental studies
   19. EPA works with states
   20.
   21.
   22.
   23.
   24.
   25.
   26.
   27.

C. Agricultural Pollution
   1. Present tillage program not universally applicable
   2. Federal priorities for agriculture are inconsistent
   3. Agricultural runoff can be controlled
   4. Herbicide use is quite high
   5. Herbicide use produces pollution
   6. Good land is eroding
   7. Overfertilization results in harm
   8. Tillage program increases pesticide use
   9.
   10.
   11.
   12.
   13.
   14.
   15.
   16. Tillage program decreases pollution
   17. Standards should not be frozen in for agricultural methods
   18. Erosion strikes marginal cropland
   19. Water Pollution Control Act applies to agriculture
   20. Alternatives to tillage exist

Blank spaces are left in the index outline to allow room for adding new categories as the number of evidence cards grows. It is far better to be too lenient in the number of blank spaces left than to leave too few and run out of space for new categories. The number of cards in each category should be kept to a *maximum* of ten. When there are more then ten cards in a category, it is time to reread the cards in that file and seriously consider subdividing the category.

The index cards (divider cards) in the evidence file are labeled with the appropriate letters and numbers. The evidence cards are labeled with the proper box numbers and subject letters and numbers. If during a debate the debater wants to prove that states cannot afford the costs of maintaining water quality, the index sheet would show that the material is filed under "A3." After the debate, the cards that were used could be quickly refiled under the "A3" heading, which would have been noted in the upper right-hand corner of the card.

Debaters who have used the index sheet system report that it is a very effective way to handle large amounts of evidence. They say that the cards can be easily filed, quickly found, and just as quickly refiled after a round. This is probably true because many index headings are possible under a code designation and because the entire subject subcategory does not have to be written on each index card and evidence card. Also, it is considerably easier to read the code than to read a lengthy heading when one is searching through a file box. A word of warning: If the debater loses the index sheets, there is no way of knowing where the evidence is filed. It would be wise to carry a duplicate or two at all times and to keep an extra at home.

Maintaining the Evidence Files

It is wise to read through your files periodically. Cards that are too general can be discarded. As your knowledge of a topic grows, the value of some cards will decrease. Sometimes, however, you will find material that you overlooked or whose value you did not recognize or understand at first. That material might suddenly become the best evidence in the file. The important thing is to extend the thinking approach to debate to the evidence file. It is not the size of the file that is important, but the quality of the evidence in the file.

Students who type all of their evidence on briefs rather than on index cards must file all materials in notebooks. Notebooks are divided into affirmative and negative materials. Affirmative notebooks are divided into sections such as first affirmative constructive, topicality responses, generic first negative responses, first affirmative rebuttal responses, and case specific responses. Negative notebooks usually separate generic arguments from case specific arguments. Case specific arguments are generally organized alphabetically, with tabs of one color separating the cases and tabs of another color separating specific arguments or blocks of arguments.

QUESTIONS FOR DISCUSSION

1. What are the two types of filing systems? What is the difference between the two? What are the advantages and/or disadvantages of each?

2. Why is it important to maintain your files?

ACTIVITIES

1. Before you can file your evidence, you must decide which filing system to use. Choose one of the two systems described in this chapter and explain your reasons for choosing it. Remember, a good filing system is the key to being able to locate evidence for use in a debate round. Your system *must* enable you to retrieve pieces of information quickly.

2. Once you have accumulated 50 pieces of evidence, you should begin filing them. Be sure to label each card for easy refiling. After filing approximately 150 pieces of evidence, read through your file to see if your evidence is filed properly. Quite often, you will reassign cards to another category as you learn more about a topic. Keeping up with your filing will also help you to determine where you need to do more research.

6

Types of Research Sources

You have a proposition for debate. You now understand how to set up a plan of research. You also know what to do with the evidence once you find it. But, where do you find the evidence? There are a number of sources. Six of them are discussed in this chapter: books, periodicals, pamphlets, newspapers, local publications, and government documents. Any of these used in isolation can probably provide sufficient evidence to support an argument. However, knowing how to research and use *each* of these sources will make your search for support (evidence) both easier and more effective. It is much like learning to cook. You can survive on sandwiches as the main course at each meal. Or, you can learn to combine a variety of ingredients and foods in interesting ways for greater satisfaction. To make your research efforts effective, you should understand the following terms:

American Statistics Index

Congressional Information Service Index

Index to Legal Periodicals

Monthly Catalog

Vertical File Index

Successful debaters know how and where to find the information that they need. Research can be done in a wide variety of sources. A solid understanding of those sources and their use can mean the difference between obtaining vital evidence and not obtaining it—between winning and not winning a debate competition. A thorough knowledge of how to use research sources results in efficient use of the debater's time and energies. In this chapter, we will look closely at various research sources, including books, periodicals, legal and government publications.

BOOKS

There are two categories of books to consider when you are doing research: (1) reference books and (2) textbooks and specialized books.

Reference Books
You should begin with reference books. These are very good for gathering background material and gaining a general understanding of the topic area. Sometimes a reference book can be an excellent place to find specific pieces of information. The following are reference books you may want to consider using. Remember, which reference books you consult will be determined by the topic you are debating. This list is not intended to be all-inclusive; it is a starting point.

Statistical Abstract of the United States. An exhaustive summary of current statistics.

Economics by Paul Samuelson. An excellent and very readable text in beginning economics.

The United States in World Affairs. Published by the Council on Foreign Relations, it provides a good history and analysis of world affairs for each year.

Editorial Research Reports. An outstanding reference series. Available only to newspapers and libraries, it presents in-depth analyses of currently important topics.

Political Handbook of the World. A good reference for specific information about foreign countries.

Yearbook of the United Nations

Yearbook of World Affairs

Britannica Book of the Year

New International Yearbook

New York Times Economic Review and Forecast. A very good review of economic development in different areas of the world.

Relations of Nations by Frederick H. Hartmann. A good examination of foreign policy and foreign relations.

Documents of International Affairs

Treaties in Force. The Department of State's annual list of all the treaties to which the United States is bound.

Legislation on Foreign Relations. By the Committee on Foreign Relations, U.S. Senate.

Annual Report of the Council of Economic Advisors. An outstanding source for an analysis of the economic problems facing the United States.

Brookings Institute Publications. A series of in-depth analyses of important issues.

Documents of American History

Black's Law Dictionary. The unquestioned standard work for legal terms and court precedents for concepts of law.

Constitutional Criminal Procedure. American Casebook Series.

American Constitution by Lockhart, Kamisar, and Choper.

Constitutional Law. Gilbert Law Summaries.

Encyclopaedia Britannica. A thorough discussion of various topics at an adult level; thought by many to be the best encyclopedia.
World Almanac
Information Please Almanac
Reader's Digest Almanac
Book of the States

Textbooks and Specialized Books   Titles of textbooks and specialized books can be found in the card catalog. Using your list of key terms, first look in the card catalog for general books and then move to the more specialized books. While you are reading these books, always be alert to new ideas and terms to add to your key terms list. From the card catalog make a bibliographical listing of books that appear to relate to the topic. Not all the books you put on your list will prove to be of value. Because you do not have an unlimited amount of time to conduct your research, carefully decide which books you will read. First, check the table of contents, the author's qualifications, and the date of publication. This information will help you decide the merits of the book. You should also pay special attention to the footnotes, the bibliography, and the index. These may direct you to other materials worth reading.

To keep abreast of newly published books, consult *Books in Print,* which is an annual listing of published books by subject, author, and title. It is supplemented by *Forthcoming Books,* a bimonthly listing of all books scheduled for publication within the next five months.

QUESTIONS FOR DISCUSSION   1. What are the two categories of books you will consult when you are doing research? What is the difference between the two?

2. What determines the value of the book for research?

3. What is *Books in Print?*

ACTIVITY   1. Using the following proposition, do a library survey of books. First, identify which reference books might be of value and why. Second, using the card catalog, make a bibliography of books that might be used for researching this proposition.

Resolved: That the United States defense budget is adequate to ensure national security.

PERIODICALS

Periodicals (magazines) are a very good source of recent evidence. Titles of articles in general-circulation periodicals, such as *Time, Newsweek, Business Week,* and *Fortune,* can be found in the *Reader's Guide to Periodical Literature.* These sources generally produce general articles and therefore general evidence. Far more valuable will be limited-circulation periodicals intended for a more specialized reading audience. Titles of articles in these periodicals can be found in special indexes. Two examples of these indexes are the *Social Sciences and Humanities Index* and *The Bulletin of the Public Affairs Information Services.* The latter index also lists important articles in general circulation periodicals, some recently published books, and major government documents.

The following is a sample of some general-circulation and limited-circulation periodicals.

General-circulation Periodicals	Limited-circulation Periodicals
Time	*The London Economist*
Newsweek	*Annals of the American Academy of*
U.S. News and World Report	*Political and Social Science*
Fortune	*Economist*
Business Week	*Chemical and Engineering News*
The New Republic	*The Reporter*
Nation's Business	*The World Today*
Saturday Review	*Food Engineering*
Science	*Commonweal*
Atlantic Monthly	*Journal of the American Medical*
Forbes	*Association*
Money	*Business and Economic Review*
The Nation	*Public Welfare*
Harper's	*Environment*
	Foreign Affairs Monthly. (An excellent source of foreign affairs material by the best authors.)
	Great Decisions. (Published annually by the Foreign Policy Association; very objective.)
	Social Science Quarterly
	Industrial Development
	Farm Journal
	Urban Education

Many high school libraries do not have some of the periodicals found in the specialized indexes. If this is the case with your library and if you cannot obtain the periodicals you need through a local university library, you can procure them in either of two ways. First, some periodicals can be obtained through interlibrary loan, a procedure by which the librarian makes arrangements to borrow materials from another library that subscribes to the specific journals requested. Second, single copies of most publications can be purchased directly from the publisher.

QUESTIONS FOR DISCUSSION

1. What guide should you consult to find general circulation periodicals?

2. When you are looking for more specialized periodicals, what can you do if the library does not carry the periodicals you need?

ACTIVITIES

1. On any given topic, some periodicals are more useful than others. Learning to identify where to begin your search can often save you a great deal of time. Using one of the propositions listed on page 34,
   a. Make a list of the more common periodicals that may provide research materials on the proposition.
   b. Moving from the general to the specific, make a list of more specialized periodicals that might contain research materials on the proposition.
   c. Using these lists as a starting point, begin your research on the proposition you have chosen. Make a bibliography of relevant sources. Make copies of at least ten of the articles to bring to class. Be prepared to explain why these articles are of value. Save the articles for a research exercise later.

2. Using the *Reader's Guide to Periodical Literature,* put together a bibliography of periodicals on the following proposition. Remember to make a list of key terms before consulting the *Reader's Guide.*

   Resolved: That the federal government should implement programs to curtail our rising unemployment.

3. Using *The Bulletin of the Public Affairs Information Service,* put together a bibliography of periodicals on the proposition in Activity 1.

4. Make a copy of ten articles from your two bibliographies. Be prepared to explain why these articles are worth researching. Save the articles for later use.

NEWSPAPERS

One of the best ways to stay abreast of current events is to read the newspaper. Your local newspaper is a good place to start. It is also a good idea to read the *New York Times,* which contains reports of Congressional committee hearings, as well as reprints of important testimony. Finally, the Sunday edition of the *New York Times* includes a special section, "News of the Week in Review," that summarizes and analyzes the news of the past week. Most libraries carry the *New York Times.* If for some reason it is not in your school library, you can find it in your local public library. The *New York Times* publishes its own semimonthly indexes, which are collected annually. The indexes are valuable not only for finding articles in the *New York Times,* but also for locating accounts of similar events printed in other newspapers on the same day.

Major news stories usually appear in all daily newspapers on approximately the same date. With the date of an article appearing in the *New York Times,* you can usually find the same story in other newspapers by looking at newspapers published two or three days before and two or three days after the date listed in the *New York Times Index.* The following are newspapers you may want to read if they are carried by your library:

London Times   *Washington Post*
Christian Science Monitor   *Chicago Tribune*
Wall Street Journal   *Los Angeles Times*

Many libraries have indexes to major local newspapers even if they do not carry the newspaper.

QUESTIONS FOR DISCUSSION

1. Why is it useful to follow the *New York Times*?

2. Why is it important to examine a daily newspaper when you are researching a proposition for debate?

ACTIVITY

1. Using the proposition you chose in Activity 1 on page 59, collect newspaper articles for the next week. You are looking for articles that have information for or against the resolution you have chosen. Look at your local newspaper, the *New York Times,* and the *Wall Street Journal.* You may also want to include the *Washington Post.* Explain why these articles are useful for researching the proposition. Save the articles for later use.

PAMPHLETS

Many pressure groups, foundations, academic departments, think tanks, and other organizations issue pamphlets, documents, and special reports. A sampling of these materials is listed in the *Vertical File Index,* which is carried by most libraries. Most libraries maintain a vertical file of pamphlets and will order materials for it on request. The *Vertical File Index* also lists organizations from which you may order pamphlets directly, sometimes free of charge. The best way to discover the identity of such groups is to pose three questions to yourself:

1. Who might be interested in this problem area?

2. Who stands to gain from the adoption of the resolution?

3. Who would lose from the adoption of this resolution?

By answering these questions you will be able to identify a number of special interest groups, most of which will be more than happy to supply you with material. However, you must analyze the information you receive from these organizations very carefully. Remember, many of these groups are not objective. The problem is not that their facts and statistics are necessarily false. It's that their *interpretations* of facts might be biased. Listed below are some examples of organizations you might want to contact for information:

Health Care

The American Medical Association
The Social Security Administration
The Pharmaceutical Manufacturers
 Association
The World Health Organization

American Public Health Association
Health Information Foundation
Health Insurance Institute

Poverty and Unemployment

Institute of Research on Poverty
Bureau of Social Science Research
Committee for Economic
 Development
AFL-CIO

Institute of Labor and Industrial
 Relations
Environmentalists for Full
 Employment
Industrial Relations Research
 Association

Pollution

Federation of American Scientists
Resources for the Future
Council on Environmental Quality

Center for Coastal and
 Environmental Studies
Sierra Club

Energy

Critical Mass
American Association for the
 Advancement of Science
National Petroleum Council
American Petroleum Institute
Geothermal Resources Council
American Power Conference

Coal Research Bureau
Exxon Corporation
Gulf Oil Corporation
American Gas Association

Other Organizations

U.S. Council on Environmental
 Quality
Department of Commerce
The Rand Corporation
U.S. General Accounting Office
Appropriations Committee, U.S.
 Senate
Brookings Institution

Institute for Policy Studies
The Bureau of National Affairs, Inc.
U.S. Department of Agriculture
International Monetary Fund
Committee for Economic
 Development

Names of organizations can also be found in bibliographies and footnotes. If you can't find the names of relevant groups in these sources, you can consult the *World Almanac,* which lists more than 25,000 organizations, or the *Encyclopedia of Associations.* The information available from such organizations may be extremely valuable in your construction of a case or in your development of a specific argument. You should also be aware of the points of view reflected in such publications. If read with caution some of these materials can be very good sources of evidence.

QUESTIONS FOR DISCUSSION

1. What is the *Vertical File Index?*

2. What three questions should you ask when you are trying to identify groups to write to for information?

3. Once you have identified the organizations you would like to write to, how can you find their addresses?

ACTIVITIES

1. Using the proposition you chose in Activity 1 on page 59, make a list of organizations that might provide you with information on the topic. Do not limit your list to the organizations suggested here. Check the *Vertical File Index.* You can also find possible sources of information by reading through the bibliographies and footnotes of articles on the topic.

2. Once you have a list of organizations, find the addresses of these organizations in the library.

3. Draft a letter to these groups explaining what you are doing as a debater and requesting any information or bibliographies they might have on the topic.

LEGAL PUBLICATIONS

Index to Legal Publications

Available at most university libraries, the *Index to Legal Periodicals* includes all law journals. It is divided into three sections. The first section is the subject and author index, which contains bibliographical information relating to articles in the law journals. Included here are some case notes, which describe particular cases. The second section provides a table of cases alphabetically listed by plaintiff's name. Thus, if the researcher would like to examine a particular case in a given year, he or she would simply look at the appropriate case name in the legal index. Third, the index also provides a book review section in which it lists, under the name of the author (or the title of the work, if the author is unknown), the review available on a particular topic.

Many journal articles listed in the *Index to Legal Periodicals* comment on specific laws and/or cases.

Legal periodicals are usually not available in general libraries. To find them you may have to consult law and bar association libraries. For your purposes there are three types of legal publications that may prove valuable.

Treatises

First, law libraries usually keep a large collection of books and pamphlets that are referred to as treatises. These are indexed in a card catalog that is similar to the catalog in a general library.

Court Decisions   Second, texts of court decisions in cases you may wish to investigate can also be found in the law library. The texts of U.S. Supreme Court decisions are given in *United States Reports,* which is available at most county courthouses. The index cites cases first by volume number, then by an abbreviated title of the book the case is found in (such as "U.S." or "Sup. Ct."), and then by the page number (and the date in parentheses). Thus, for *Lockner* v. *New York,* the citation reads "198 U.S. 45," which indicates that the case can be found in volume 198 of the *U.S. Reports,* page 45.

But it is not always necessary to wait until the text of the U.S. Supreme Court case is actually bound in one of the Supreme Court volumes in order to read it. Instead, there are other sources for finding current Supreme Court cases. For example, the *New York Times* frequently prints the entire text of a Supreme Court case the day after the decision has been released. Thus, you can gain quick access to a court case by consulting the *New York Times Index.* Also, the *Supreme Court Bulletin,* which is available at most university libraries, prints summaries of Supreme Court decisions the week after they are made.

It is important to remember that the sources described above are only for U.S. Supreme Court decisions. Frequently, an investigator will need to find information relating to lower court decisions. Material relating to federal district courts is published in the *Federal Supplement,* which is cited as "F. Sup." or "F.S." State court decisions are rendered in a regional reporting system, which takes the form of a series of different accumulations. For example, *Atlantic Reporter* discusses decisions in Delaware, Maryland, New Hampshire, New Jersey, and nearby states. *The Southern Reporter, The Northeastern, The Northwestern, The Pacific, The Southeastern,* and *Southwestern Reports* report cases from state courts in designated areas. All of these cases are reported in the same basic form, indicating the volume of the case, the source cited (whether it be *Atlantic Reporter, Federal Supplement, U. S. Reports,* etc., and the page number.

For clarification of actual decisions (the implications of the ruling or the current state of the law), you can consult *Corpus Juris Secundum,* a reference work that is available not only at law libraries, but also at major courthouses and at many general libraries. The Lawyer's Annotated Edition of *United States Reports* also includes annotations and commentaries that may be helpful.

To find a federal law, the best source is the *U. S. Code Annotated,* a series of red bound books with the initials U. S. C. A. on the binding. The researcher should first consult the index, note the volume and section in which the law can be found, and then find the appropriate volume and section. One word of caution is necessary. Frequently, the *U. S. Code Annotated* and several other of the U. S. Judicial Documents are not updated in a normal manner. Rather, in the back of the book is an insert which will update both the index and the appropriate section of the law. Thus, if looking for a recent law, it may be necessary to look at the back pocket of the book to find that law. This is true as well for Supreme Court decisions.

Legal Periodicals   The third type of legal publication is the legal periodical. There are two principal kinds of legal journals. First, professional societies or groups publish journals containing material pertinent to their special interests. Examples are the *Journal of World Trade Law* and the *Journal of International Law and Economics.* Second, most of the nation's law schools publish law reviews. Law reviews usually are divided into two parts. The front section contains articles by judges, law professors, and practicing attorneys. These articles provide broad treatment of legal problems and should be read with great care. The back section, often titled "Notes" or "Comments," should be approached with some caution.

These sections, written by student editors of the journal, focus on new court rulings and discuss current problems in the law. Several law reviews frequently include comments pertinent to the case. Because some of these reviews occasionally cover the same issues or cases, it may be unnecessary to read them all. Finally, unsigned citations to law reviews usually refer to the student-written "Notes" section.

QUESTIONS FOR DISCUSSION

1. Describe the three sections of the *Index to Legal Periodicals.*

2. How would you go about finding information on the U.S. Supreme Court decision in *Lockner v. New York*?

3. If you do not want to wait for the *U.S. Reports* to be released on a particular case, how else can you find out about the case?

4. For clarification of an actual decision one can consult _____.

5. Describe how to use the *U.S. Code Annotated* to find a federal law.

6. What are the two sections of articles in most law reviews? Why are the articles in the front section more useful than those in the "Notes" or "Comments" section?

ACTIVITIES

1. Using the proposition you chose in Activity 1 on page 59, begin researching legal periodicals. Most school and local libraries carry the index to legal periodicals even if they do not carry the periodicals themselves. Make a bibliography of sources relevant to your topic.

2. Individually or as a class, visit a library that has legal periodicals. After reading several of the articles listed in your bibliography, copy two of them and bring them back to class for use in a later research exercise.

GOVERNMENT DOCUMENTS

Government documents can provide valuable information. On most topics they can be a direct source of information, as well as a major summary source for materials that are difficult to obtain directly. Special reports, for example, typically contain the results of commissioned studies, which may not be available elsewhere. The annual report of many of the executive agencies of the federal government may also prove useful. *The Federal Bureau of Investigation Uniform Crime Reports* is valuable if you are doing research on crime. If you are researching a health care topic, you might want to examine the *Task Force on Medicaid and Related Programs.*

Congressional hearings and reports will be especially good sources of evidence. Listed below are committees whose reports you might want to look at.

Poverty

House Committee on Education and Labor

Senate Committee on Labor and Public Welfare

Senate Committee on Government Operations

House Committee on Ways and Means

Senate Committee on Finance

Joint Economic Committee

Joint Committee on Education and Labor

Pollution

House Committee on Environment and Public Works

Senate Committee on Environment and Public Works

House Committee on Public Works and Transportation

House Committee on Ways and Means

Senate Committee on Finance

Joint Economic Committee

Committee on Science and Technology

House Committee on Agriculture

House Committee on Government Operations

Senate Subcommittee on Toxic Substances and Environmental Oversight

House Subcommittee on Water Resources

Crime

House and Senate Judiciary Committees

House Internal Security Committee

House Select Committee on Crime

House Subcommittee on Criminal Justice

Health Care

House Appropriations Committee

House Interstate and Foreign Commerce Committee

House Ways and Means Committee

Senate Labor and Public Welfare Committee

Energy

House Committee on Interior and Insular Affairs

House Committee on Science and Technology

House Subcommittee on Energy and Power

Senate Committee on Governmental Affairs

Senate Committee on Commerce

Senate Committee on Science and Transportation

Senate Foreign Affairs Committee

Senate Committee on Energy and Natural Resources

Congressional Quarterly   To remain knowledgeable about current developments in congressional committees, you should frequently consult the *Congressional Quarterly*—a weekly résumé of activities in Congress. The calendars of these committees, which list the most recent committee publications and scheduled hearings, may be obtained free of charge, along with single copies of the transcripts or hearings, by writing either the chairperson of the committee or your senator or representative.

When researching congressional hearings, you will quickly discover that the transcripts are voluminous. It would be impossible to read everything. Nor would it be worth your time to read everything. It is necessary to select with care those sections that are especially worthy of attention. You should concentrate primarily on the statements of professors and professionals from such fields as sociology, pathology, toxicology, medicine, political science, economics, chemistry, and the law; representatives of academic research bureaus, technical organizations, and pertinent government agencies; and the directors of reputable foundations or groups.

You can save time if you realize that hearings are often repetitious. The same witnesses may give almost identical statements at different hearings concerning the same problem. There may even be repetition within the same hearing. Frequently, a witness reads a prepared statement aloud and then has the written version of his or her statement included in the record.

The dialogue between witnesses and committee members following the witnesses' formal statements should not be overlooked. This interchange often is a source of excellent information, particularly of qualifications or of limitations that witnesses may have forgotten to place on their overly generalized preliminary remarks.

Finally, the reports of the committees, printed after the conclusion of the hearings, are also worthy of attention. Although the reports often duplicate the hearings, they contain many ideas and opinions not presented in the original hearings.

Agency Publications   Individual publications of executive agencies represent still another type of government document. While some agencies, such as the Department of Agriculture, publish valuable pamphlets and reports, one should be wary of propagandistic publicity pieces that are used by some agencies primarily as promotional items—leaflets, brochures, and handouts. Single copies of specific government agency publications generally can be obtained by writing directly to the issuing agency. It is a good idea to request, at the same time, a bibliography of related materials published by the same agency. The bibliography may contain publications not listed elsewhere.

Congressional Record   It is always possible to find unexpected evidence in the *Congressional Record,* the final type of government document. Unless one has virtually unlimited research time, however, reading the *Record* should be given a low priority. Many of the reprints in the *Record* are letters or editorials from obscure local newspapers. Should a debater cite evidence from a newspaper or periodical, however, one's best chance of locating it is to peruse the *Record* for ten or fifteen days following the newspaper or periodical date cited. It usually can be found.

Congressional   Because each year over 300 congressional committees and subcommittees
Information   publish over 800,000 pages of information, the debate researcher must be
Service Index   able to gain access to this vital information. The *Congressional Information Service Index (CIS)* makes much of that material accessible. The *CIS Index* is published each month, with annual bound accumulations and a five-year multiple cumulative index. Each of the indexes is divided into two basic sections. The first is the abstract section.

Abstract section   In the abstract section is a description of each individual publication organized by *CIS* accession number. The first letter in the accession number stands for the parent body issuing the document or report. H stands for the House, J for a joint committee, and S for the Senate. The remaining two numbers, which are assigned to the committees in alphabetical order, identify the committee of origin. For example, materials coming from the Senate Finance Committee are numbered S36. A final digit is added to the committee code to indicate the publication type:

0 = House or Senate Document or Special Publication
1 = Hearing
2 = Committee Print
3 = House or Senate Report
4 = Senate Executive Report
5 = Senate Executive Document

Following this system, then, S361 = a Senate Finance Committee hearings volume. Every abstract number begins with a similar four-character code, followed by a dash and a serial number. Thus, S361–24 = the twenty-fourth volume of hearings from the Senate Finance Committee abstracted during a given year. In the case of hearings testimony abstracts, a decimal number is added to identify each individual item of testimony. Thus, S361–24.1 = the first item of testimony abstracted in this volume of hearings.

Since the organizational system stays the same from year to year and the committees designated by the organization are consistent, it makes no difference what year is being examined. The citation S361 always refers to Senate Finance Committee hearings. Therefore, it is sometimes easier to look in the appropriate year and the appropriate committee to find the material emanating from that committee in that year. Frequently an incomplete citation is heard or read—for example, that Senator Jones testified in front of the Senate Finance Committee. The researcher who is comfortable with the CIS can just take that information and use the abstract to find the section where Senator Jones testified before the Senate Finance Committee without having to look through a whole series of other documents. This makes research very simple.

Following the accession number in the abstract section is an abstract of the cited material. This abstract is designed to summarize the subject matter, to indicate the nature and page range locations of the potentially useful materials included in the publication, and to provide enough details to enable a researcher to decide accurately whether the document is useful and worth the trip to the stacks.

The *CIS* also provides public law abstracts and their legislative histories. These might include references to documents, usually presidential messages, requesting or opposing legislation, hearings often held first to discuss subject matter and the need for legislation and subsequently to consider specific proposed legislation, and reports and conference reports on various bills involved in the evolution of the law's enactment. So, for the researcher who needs to examine previous legislation these public law histories can be very important.

Index section   In the index volume or index section of the *CIS,* the researcher can find an index to all the abstracts. Essentially there are four indexes within the index section. The first part of the index is Subjects and Names. Within this index all the subjects and the names of those people testifying in the abstracts are organized for the researcher. "See Also" references are included. Supplementary indexes provide direct access to abstracts though knowledge of the title of a publication, the number of a bill, report, document, or the name of a committee or subcommittee chairman. Normally, using the *CIS* is a four-step process:

1. Search the index to identify publications of interest.

2. Note the accession numbers of relevant abstracts.

3. Locate and review the abstracts to evaluate the contents of the publication.

4. Obtain the publications for complete reference. Many of these publications are available in any library that has the *CIS Index* available. Publications marked by a bullet are sent to depository libraries. High school students can usually use such libraries, but they often need a special visitor's pass in order to check out materials such as government documents. Students should check with their high school librarian and obtain such a pass, if required, before traveling to the library.

5. If the document cannot be located in the stacks of the library, ask the reference librarian for help. It may be available on microfiche. Anything listed in the *CIS* is available in some way. For the entries in which a price is indicated in the abstract, the publications in print rather than microfiche can be purchased from the Superintendent of Documents, Washington, D.C. 20402. Publications for which no price is indicated frequently can be obtained by writing to the issuing committee or subcommittee. It is advisable that an address label also be included. These can be sent to the Senate committees at Washington, D. C. 20512 and the House committees at Washington, D. C. 20515. Documents marked by a dagger are usually available in limited quantities from the issuing committee. Those marked with a double dagger are printed for official use and are not available for general distribution. Those marked with a diamond are specifically designated by the issuing committee as not for distribution. A microfiche copy of any item listed in *CIS* can be purchased from the *CIS*. Not only does the *CIS Index* provide the researcher with an extremely valuable source of information but virtually opens up access to all congressional information at a reasonable price to the researcher. The only significant weakness to *CIS* is that it does not include executive branch publications or court decisions.

American Statistics Index   The *American Statistics Index* is a monthly abstract and index publication with annual cumulations. It covers all statistical publications of the U. S. government, including congressional publications with substantial statistical data. The *ASI*/Microfiche Library and *ASI* Documents-on-Demand services provide full-text availability of *ASI* publications in a manner paralleling *CIS*/Index microfiche services. Detailed information on how to use the index is included at the beginning of each publication.

Monthly Catalog   In addition to the *CIS Index* another government publication that indexes government documents is the *Monthly Catalog of United States Publication*. The *Monthly Catalog* is especially useful for finding out about executive department publications because these are not indexed in the *CIS Index*. As with most government indexes, the *Monthly Catalog* uses essentially a two-part system for finding the appropriate information. The researcher uses the accession number in the subject section to find a specific abstract reference in the front of the catalog. The abstract reference gives the shelf number needed to find the document in the stacks. It is important to note the number of the pages in a document. Frequently, government documents are so short that it may be not worth the time to look them up.

Government documents are classified by issuing agency. For example, HE are the letters for the Department of Health, J stands for the Justice Department, IN stands for the Interior Department, and Y is for Congressional General Service Administration topics. PR EX is on all documents issued by the President. If you find you are using publications of a certain agency often, it may be faster to check through the abstracts. Generally, you will begin research by using the subject index section. Entries will end with an accession number. This number is usually fairly short, for example—76–5149. Use this number to obtain a complete citation in the abstracts section. The accession number will be at the left-hand top of the entry. This number will be followed in the central column by the shelf number. This number is usually fairly long—e.g., HE 20.4102:G 58/2. It is important to correctly copy letters, numbers, periods, colons, and slashes in order to find the document in the stacks.

QUESTIONS FOR DISCUSSION

1. Explain how to use the *Congressional Information Service Index.*

2. Explain how to use the *American Statistics Index.*

3. Why are congressional hearings of value for research?

4. Should one spend a great of time reading the *Congressional Record*? Why or why not?

5. How does one use the *Monthly Catalog of United States Publications*? What kinds of information are indexed here?

ACTIVITIES

1. Using the *Monthly Catalog of United States Government Publications,* put together a bibliography of citations on the proposition chosen on page 59. Also, consult the *Congressional Quarterly* or the *Bulletin of the Public Affairs Information Service* for the most recent document releases. Draft a letter to your congressperson explaining what you are doing as a debater and request copies of the most relevant government documents on your list. Documents can also be requested directly from the department or committee involved. Try writing to two or three committees for information. Include a couple of the citations you have found and ask for additional information. You can also write to the Superintendent of Documents, but there is usually a charge for documents.

2. Now try making a bibliography using the *Congressional Information Service Index.* Continue with the *American Statistics Index.*

7

The Affirmative Position

Knowing how to debate the affirmative is a valuable lifeskill. You can apply the skill in a variety of ways: to argue for a change in curfew, use of the family car, a variance in school policy, a promotion. Arguing for change takes skill and practice. It requires careful, thorough thinking to present good reasons for change and a plan of action that would be beneficial to all involved parties. If you want to use the family car, for example, you must give convincing reasons why you should be allowed to borrow it. To effectively debate the affirmative, you need to understand the following key terms:

case	harm
comparative advantage case	inherency
contention	need-plan case
definition of terms	significance
disadvantages	solvency
discretionary powers	stock issues

The affirmative argues for the proposition. To begin, consider the basic logic of affirmative debating. The state of public affairs is considered to be a mixed situation. There are many good programs and some bad ones. There are needs that the government has taken care of and needs that have been neglected. Some programs are good. Others need to be overhauled or eliminated. The world of public policy is imperfect. Reasonable discussion and debate can identify possible improvements in the existing state of affairs. The affirmative acts as an advocate (agent) for changing the present system. In debate we often refer to the present system as the status quo. The direction and type of change that the affirmative must advocate is identified by the proposition.

For these reasons, the affirmative shoulders the burden of proof. The affirmative maintains that there is sufficient evidence to indicate that a part of the present system has failed or is failing and that the proposition can serve as a remedy for the failure. If there is no harm to present policy, no defect in need of correction, then there is no reason to change. In addition, even if there is a problem, if the plan is unworkable or impractical, there is no reason for change.

Even though the affirmative has shown that the present system is defective and that the defect can be remedied by the proposition, it has another obligation. The affirmative case for change must be compelling enough to overcome presumption. As a rule, presumption says that the affirmative case establishes a reason (justification) for change. Even if the affirmative proves that there is a need for change and that the proposed change will work, the arguments must constitute a justification for change.

BASIC AFFIRMATIVE CONCEPTS

It is necessary to define several important terms before we examine how the affirmative position is debated.

Topicality It is the responsibility of the affirmative to choose an area within the proposition. This is sometimes referred to as the intent of the proposition.

Definition of Terms The affirmative has the obligation to define terms so that the nature of the action advocated is clear to everyone concerned. Definitions can be made by quoting experts who use the terms in a special way, by referring to dictionaries to suggest common usage, or by referring to examples of common usage.

The Contention A *contention* is a claim made by the affirmative or the negative. Most often, a contention is a single, declarative statement. Sometimes the proposition being debated is called the main contention because it is the major claim of the affirmative. Typically, the affirmative contends that there is a harm, that it is significant, that it is inherent, that the plan will solve the harm, and that there are positive side effects to the plan. Other affirmative statements are subcontentions. (In debate, however, any major affirmative claim is simply called a contention.)

Reasoning and Proof To meet the burden of proof, however, the affirmative cannot merely assert contentions. They must be supported with reasoning and proof. Proof is the evidence introduced to support the claim. Reasoning explains why the evidence supports the specific claim in question. To prove the contention that bureaucracy is inefficient, one might introduce evidence of delays and mistakes characteristic of certain administrations. This constitutes evidence. Reasoning must be used to connect the evidence to the general claim. Thus, one might reason that delays and mistakes of a sufficient number and severity can be said to constitute inefficiency. The contentions should be always accompanied by a well-organized presentation of evidence and reasoning.

Stock Issues

Stock issues are the basis of major affirmative contentions. Stock issues are claims that affirmatives must make in order to present a prima facie case. Each stock issue must be supported by reasoning and evidence. Stock issues include:

Harm. Is there a problem in the status quo that can be said to merit the attention of policy makers?

Significance. Is the problem important enough to take the time and energy of policy makers?

Inherency. Does the problem inhere in the policies pursued by the status quo?

Solvency. Will the affirmative plan solve the purported problem?

Disadvantages. These are a stock issue, but the negative has the obligation to present them. The affirmative need not negate all possible disadvantages if it fulfills its initial burden of proof.

Affirmative Case

The *affirmative case* is composed of the definition of terms, plan, and stock issues. The affirmative case is presented in its complete form by the first affirmative constructive and extended by the second speaker. To win a debate, the affirmative must sustain support for a substantial part of its case against negative attacks. Although affirmative case formats vary, the obligations for establishing the resolution are relatively similar.

You must be familiar with these basic terms and concepts to debate. In the next section of the chapter, we will study these concepts in greater detail.

Affirmative Plan

The *affirmative plan* is the mechanism used by the affirmative to enact the proposition. A plan is structured around several planks. The planks identify who enforces the plan, what is to be done, and how the procedures are to be carried out. A plan can be quite detailed when the procedure to be followed is complicated by multiple options. A plan can be simple if the affirmative so wishes.

QUESTIONS FOR DISCUSSION

1. The affirmative has the duty to _____.

2. Why is it important for an affirmative case to be topical?

3. What is the difference between reasoning and proof?

DEFINING THE TERMS OF THE PROPOSITION

The nature and quality of propositions differ. Ideally, a proposition on a policy topic ought to specify a clear direction for a particular policy. Consider a good proposition: Resolved: That the United States should guarantee a minimum annual cash income for all American citizens. This proposition explains who should do the action, what the action should be, and for whom the action should be done. There is little ambiguity requiring definition. However, not all propositions are so clear cut. If the proposition calls for the federal government to adopt a comprehensive farm policy in the United States, it is unclear what should be done. Indeed, even the definition of the word *farm* is disputable.

Frequently, the first affirmative constructive does not spend a significant amount of time defining terms. If the proposition is reasonably constructed and if most debaters are familiar with the proposition, the issue may not be viewed as important. However, the affirmative must be prepared to defend its definitions. Since the negative can win the debate by proving that the affirmative has misconstrued the proposition significantly, the affirmative is always vulnerable to topicality attacks [those arguments that suggest that the affirmative has not met the burdens imposed by the proposition or has exceeded policy sanctioned by the proposition]. The second affirmative constructive speaker should prepare briefs to argue for the validity of the affirmative definitions.

When the proposition is imprecise or where it uses terms that may have multiple meanings, understanding the wording of the proposition becomes important. There are several ways to do this.

Common Usage

A common dictionary is a guide to the meanings of a policy resolution. A common definition is often desirable because policy making ought to reflect the concerns of the everyday citizen rather than a special interest group or person. The problem with dictionary definitions, however, is that they may lack the necessary precision. The word *comprehensive* may be ordinarily defined as "thoroughgoing" or "complete," but such a definition lends little insight into the kind of action mandated by the proposition mentioned above.

Experts

Special dictionaries can be consulted for specific terms pertaining to such fields of policy research as economics, the law, and political science. Expert definitions are often more precise than common ones, and they can help to clarify seemingly vague terms. A dictionary definition of *land use* would probably refer to any activity that is terrestrial in nature. In the field of ecology, however, *land use* is more restrictively defined, and refers to soil erosion and pollution. If the common definition unreasonably broadens the resolution, an expert definition may make the terms more exact and the topic more manageable.

Operational Definition

This method of defining terms is based on the affirmative plan as an instance enactment of the proposition. If the proposition requires a "comprehensive program," then the plan is offered as an example of what such a comprehensive policy might look like.

Use of Example

Definition by example is similar to operational definition. Its major characteristic is that the affirmative relies on diverse examples in which the term has been applied to similar policies and argues by analogy (comparison) that the term is appropriate. If environmental protection legislation has been used to refer to land and water pollution, but not to air pollution specifically, then the definition of terms for a topic requiring environmental protection may legitimately leave out air pollution concerns. Definition by example is a powerful argument.

1. What are the differences among the four types of definition?

ACTIVITY 1. Using the example below define the terms of the proposition by common usage, experts, and example.

> **Resolved:** That the federal government should implement a comprehensive long-term agricultural policy in the United States.

STOCK ISSUES

Stock issues are the broad questions within a proposition. The major focus of any affirmative case is on providing evidence and reasoning to support them. Each stock issue is supported by analysis that identifies claims and provides proof. These statements are the major points of disagreement in the debate.

Harm A harm is a problem caused by the presence or absence of government policy. Collective patterns of behavior are said to present a social problem when the behavior of some people results in the harming of others. Activity that results in the unnecessary deprivation of life, liberty, or the pursuit of happiness is a social harm. Conduct, whether by private corporations or by government, that violates basic rights of liberty, freedom, equality, and association are not to be tolerated, unless justified. To some people these rights extend to material freedoms—freedom from hunger, unemployment, disease, inadequate education, and discrimination. In other societies such unjustified intrusions might not be considered social harms. In the United States, however, violations of these values are considered to be harmful.

The proposition often points to the area of harm to be discussed. If the proposition identifies policy pertaining to education, then the harm area must reside in the inadequacy of schooling and the resulting lack of knowledge and skills. If the resolution identifies policy pertaining to the environment, then one can expect to discuss the problems of ecological pollution. If the proposition points to food policy, then harms of malnutrition and starvation will be argued. In each area, the affirmative must discover the effect of the harms suggested by the proposition. Such effects may not always be straightforward. Poor education may lead to poverty, and poverty to civil unrest. Poor environmental policy may lead to ecological pollution, and pollution to the threat of extinction. Inadequate agricultural policy may lead to hunger, and hunger to a loss of human resources necessary to solve ecological problems. The important point is that the affirmative should examine the wider aspects of the harm suggested by the proposition. The wider dimensions of the problem might suggest important case areas.

1. Define harm and social harm.

ACTIVITIES 1. Identify social harms to be found in your community.

2. Outline what possible harms might be included in the proposition chosen on page 59.

Significance   The stock issue of significance is sometimes treated as part of the harm question. Indeed, even if the affirmative can isolate some undesirable policy, it still must show that the effects of the policy are substantial enough to justify consideration. Significance may be established by qualitative considerations, quantitative considerations, or both.

The affirmative establishes that a harm merits consideration from a qualitative standpoint by pointing out that the present policy (or lack of policy) violates core values. If the problem is comprised of conduct so outrageous to fundamental values of human decency, then it may not matter if there are a large number of instances of the problem. For instance, many fewer people are killed each year by state executions of prisoners than by traffic accidents, but state imposition of a death penalty deliberately takes life away from citizens. If it can be established that the state does not have the right to take away life, then the death penalty per se stands as a repugnant policy—even if only one person is executed. To the extent that the affirmative can define core values and show that a policy violates what is important to a civilized society, it establishes the qualitative significance of a harm.

The affirmative establishes that a harm merits consideration from a quantitative standpoint by presenting a large number of examples of the harm. Typically, this is accomplished by referring to empirical data. If the contention suggests that smoking is harmful, then the greater the numbers of deaths and illnesses linked to smoking, the more solid the affirmative proof. Empirical evidence is important to establish that the harm is widespread. The affirmative may wish to introduce trend evidence that suggests that the number of cases is increasing. Combined with the affirmative's reasons for change, such proof suggests that the problem will grow worse in the future.

Note that arguing for the significance of a problem can be very complex. If the harm takes on more than one form, then the affirmative must develop several subcontentions in the harm area. If the affirmative problem area identifies the ill effects of poverty, then it may be necessary to identify the number of homeless and the problems of migrancy, the number of undernourished and the problems of starvation, the number of uneducated and the problems associated with discrimination. Identifying the multiple dimensions of a harm increases the chances of establishing the overall impact of the problem.

QUESTIONS FOR DISCUSSION
1. Why must the harm be significant?

2. What are the two types of significance? Explain the difference between the two.

ACTIVITIES
1. Identify one of the harms in Activity 2 on page 74 and begin research to document the harm and its significance. Bring the information to class.

2. Write a three-minute speech developing a single harm contention.

Inherency   The affirmative must do more than prove that a harm exists. It must also establish that the problem is intrinsic to the operating procedure of the present system. To accomplish this task the affirmative must locate the causes of the problem and show that the causes cannot be eliminated by anything short of the proposition. In doing this, the affirmative establishes a unique rationale for the adoption of the policy. If the harms will go away of their own accord, then there is no real reason to change policy.

Gaps in the present system One way to establish inherency is to identify a *gap* in the laws and programs of the present system. From time to time, there arise problems that the present system did not anticipate. Groups of people may have been left out and are in need of protection. A good example of such an inherency position can be found in civil rights arguments. The United States Constitution originally guaranteed rights to American citizens but did not specifically include voting rights for American women and for black Americans. There was a gap in the present system regarding the protection of civil rights. As Americans in the 20th century gradually came to see women and blacks as deprived citizens, these gaps became noticeable, and the system had to be changed.

Set of barriers Another way to establish inherency is to point out that present policy comprises a *set of barriers* to the elimination of the harm. Let's look again at the civil rights issue. Even though women and blacks got the right to vote in the early 20th century, the manner of voting was left up to each state. The rules were discriminatory. Sometimes they required payment of poll taxes by people who were too poor to buy food and literacy tests of people who could not read. Present system rules and regulations constituted a barrier to participation in government, even though the present system nominally had filled in the gap by constitutional change. If the government chooses an inappropriate method to enact its own commitments, then that method creates a barrier to successful change.

Private sector Inherency arguments may focus on the private sector rather than on the government, as a further look at the civil rights issue shows. The real problem of inequality may reside not so much in how government acts, but in how special incentives in the private sector enforce racism. If communities benefit by keeping black residents in a subservient status, then the problem of racism may be a part in the present system. Indeed, this was the case for many years. Black workers did not have to be paid average wages for their work. Employment discrimination was legal. Moreover, because blacks lacked money they could not develop their own stores and had to buy from the white owners and landholders who benefited from their purchases. Because discrimination was accepted, the white community did not have to provide the schools, meeting places, health care or other goods and services that might have improved the conditions of the minority. If the affirmative can establish that a powerful dominant group profits from the subordination of a minority, then the problem can be said to exist in the present system.

Other examples Many inherency arguments are not as dramatic as those furnished by problems of social discrimination. Often the reasons that government policy creates gaps and barriers are worded in terms of inefficiency, duplication, waste, and inertia. Government policies are frequently the product of compromise. They grow because of lack of action. Different political administrations emphasize some programs and deemphasize others. The result is conflicting rules and regulations. Indeed, some affirmative approaches to a topic may call for the elimination of government activity in a special policy arena. For instance, if the topic called for a comprehensive farm policy, one way to put the plan into action is to deregulate farm prices. The idea is that the free market would provide a more efficient system of supply than does government subsidies. In this instance, the cause of the farm problem is said to reside in government interference in the marketplace. Similarly, in debating a topic on law enforcement, an affirmative might wish to withdraw the government's prerogative to tap private telephone lines because such activity needlessly intrudes on personal liberties. The inherency in this case is the discretionary power of government agents coupled with their power to use any system of surveillance available. The idea is that case by case decision making on wire tapping is too uncertain to guarantee rights.

In sum, the affirmative must be able to isolate the cause of the problem. If the cause is found to be a part of the current policy, then it is said to be inherent. Current policy can be found to be intrinsically defective because it does not do the job it should, thereby permitting social problems to grow. Current policy can also be defective because it causes problems that would not otherwise exist. In the first instance, the affirmative plan would remedy the harm by adding a program that would reduce the social problem. In the second instance, the affirmative plan would remedy the harm by banning unwarranted government activity. In many instances, the affirmative supports the repeal of bad laws and the expansion or addition of good ones.

QUESTIONS FOR DISCUSSION

1. Has the affirmative proven inherency if there are possible solutions to the problem in the present system?

2. What are the two ways to establish inherency? Describe the differences between the two.

ACTIVITIES

1. Using the harm isolated in Activity 2 on page 75, outline the inherent causes of the harm. Find evidence to support your claims.

2. Write a four-minute speech with a single contention, including inherency arguments.

Solvency

Solvency refers to the ability of the plan to solve a problem or bring about an advantage. There are many different reasons why the affirmative might fail to demonstrate solvency. In this section, we will discuss the method of providing plausible support for solvency. The principle the debater ought to keep in mind is one of proportion. The solvency arguments should be proportional to the problems described in establishing inherency. For every problem a remedy must be suggested.

Will a program work?

Most academic debate propositions are about questions of national importance. It is difficult to establish that sweeping changes will have positive effects unless such changes have been tried in other situations. The basic affirmative solvency argument usually works by analogy (comparison). If the program was successful on a smaller scale or at a different time or place, then—unless there are significant differences—it ought to work at a national level. Indeed, sometimes a national program might be even more successful than a local one. For example, a national hand gun ban might work even better than local bans because people could not simply walk into another town where the ban was not in effect and buy hand guns.

Pilot programs usually provide sources of information that suggest new possibilities for national programs. Traditionally, state and local governments have been known as the laboratory of democracy. It is easy to experiment with ideas at lower levels of government because decisions affect fewer lives and the programs cost less. Child care, housing, education, and other programs have been significantly influenced by policies developed at the local level. However, the affirmative must make sure that the reasons a program worked are not unique to a small program in a local area. Some pilot projects work because volunteers are very supportive of the program and the clientele for the project are specially screened to enhance the chances of success. The affirmative must be able to prove that the same success of the program could happen at the national level.

National programs in existence in the past but presently ignored or repealed offer a rich source of solvency evidence. Many of these programs were established to deal with particular problems and were ignored or repealed when the problem diminished or disappeared. One such program is public works. In times of recession every president in modern times has given in to the pressure to spend money on government jobs. Solvency evidence might be garnered by seeing which public works programs were successful and which were not. By using past examples for solvency evidence the affirmative can also identify past mistakes and take measures in the plan to avoid them.

Will a program change attitudes? A major cause of social problems in general resides in the interests of groups to perpetuate the present system. Poor people remain poor because there are others who benefit from high ghetto store prices, paying below the minimum wage, busting unions, denying credit to blighted areas, and so on. The military attracts trillions of dollars, despite having thousands upon thousands of powerful nuclear weapons, because many states and localities profit from military expenditures. In these examples, the key to solvency is changing the social structure so that incentives are directed toward what the affirmative believes to be positive social policy. A plan might penalize those who exploit the poor and thus make exploitation unprofitable. A plan might require that military expenditures be dispursed throughout all fifty states so that no regional coalition of political power would gain much from military spending.

In the absence of an altered structure of incentives, a problem might continue because the plan is circumvented by the people it is designed to control. A *circumvention* argument, made by the negative, says that the policy will have no effect, despite its good intentions, because its intent will not be obeyed. Often, the affirmative inherency evidence suggests the possibilities for circumvention. For example, the affirmative might argue that current environmental legislation is failing because business lobbies influence conservative politicians. Thus, unless the link between influence and enforcement can be broken, there is no reason to believe that the same cooptation problems would not exist under the new plan. To avoid cooptation the affirmative would have to demonstrate that a new combination of punishments and rewards would significantly reduce or eliminate influence peddling.

QUESTIONS FOR DISCUSSION

1. What does *solvency* mean?

2. What role do pilot programs play in proving solvency?

3. If the problem is an attitudinal one, how does one prove solvency?

Disadvantages

The affirmative can talk about the stock issue of harm from another perspective. Rather than emphasizing the problems inherent in the present system, the affirmative can concentrate on the benefits of altering it. The affirmative must still show that the benefits gained by the affirmative plan are unique, but the focus of argument is on the comparative advantages of adopting the proposition. Whereas the affirmative may or may not choose to argue about comparative advantages, it must always be prepared to defeat negative disadvantages.

A *disadvantage* is a claim that the proposal will result in making harmful conditions worse or in creating new harms. The negative typically argues disadvantages as part of its attack on the plan in the second negative constructive. Since the affirmative does not know exactly what disadvantages will be argued, the first affirmative speech discusses only the positive reasons for adopting the resolution. It would be a waste of time to argue against objections to the plan that may not appear in the round of debate. This section will concentrate on developing responses to disadvantages.

Is the disadvantage unique?

It clearly isn't if a harmful condition is going to come about regardless of whether the affirmative plan is adopted. In such a case, it does not matter—for purposes of evaluating the worth of the proposal—whether the plan is one among several contributing causes of the disadvantage. If a negative argues that spending money on a plan will break up the consensus on deficit reduction, the affirmative can eliminate this disadvantage merely by saying that because other programs are going to spend money, the consensus will be broken up in any case. The harmful condition must be the exclusive result of the affirmative's proposal and not the result of other factors.

Is the disadvantage significant?

If the plan is only one of many contributing factors to a future harm, then it is the responsibility of the negative to quantify the effects of the plan on the alleged harm. For example, it might be argued that giving money to the "freedom fighters" in Nicaragua will be destabilizing and likely to increase the chances of war. If those chances are already high, however, then a small increase will not really matter. Just as the affirmative has a burden to quantify the amount of harm it can eliminate (or the amount of advantage its plan can obtain), the negative has a burden to quantify the amount of harm (or disadvantage) the affirmative will create.

Present system harm vs. disadvantages

For a disadvantage to count significantly against the affirmative plan, it must have harmful social effects that are substantially greater than the harms eliminated or minimized by the affirmative plan. An analogy to the side effects of taking medicine is a good example for this. If you take medicine to cure a disease, you might have some incidental side effects—a headache or an upset stomach. If the disease is harmful, however, you are willing to take the medicine in spite of the problems created by your body's response to the drug. With very serious diseases, the side effects may be substantial, but a comparative judgment demands that the medicine be taken—otherwise, the disease might be fatal. The same logic applies to disadvantages. If the harm of the disadvantage is not as great as that eliminated by the affirmative, the policy deserves acceptance. The disadvantages may occur, but, because they are comparatively less important than the advantages, they do not undermine the affirmative's case.

Summary   In summary, the affirmative must be familiar with issues of harm, significance, inherency, solvency, and disadvantages. To advocate a change successfully, an affirmative case must be able to win the telling arguments that support each stock issue.

QUESTIONS FOR DISCUSSION

1. What is a *disadvantage*?

2. What does it mean for the disadvantage to be unique? Why must the disadvantage be unique?

3. To what extent must a disadvantage be significant?

4. Why should the affirmative compare the disadvantages to the advantages offered by the plan?

AFFIRMATIVE PLAN

The affirmative plan is presented typically in the first constructive speech. It may be presented at the beginning, middle, or end of the speech, depending on case format.

Sometimes a plan is quite simple. If a proposition calls for the elimination of a policy, then the plan need consist only of the statement that government should no longer pursue a given action. More often, however, the affirmative plan is quite complex. It must provide for a complete method of enacting the resolution. Thus, it must specify who will enforce the plan, what action must be taken, what provisions must be made to assure adequate funding and access to resources, and circumstances that might prove sufficient for exemption to normal operation. For example, on the agricultural topic, the affirmative might choose to continue government subsidies for particular crops. This is usually done to avoid a significant disadvantage to the plan.

The plan has a number of different planks. A plan plank is a statement of action to be taken. Sometimes the action is directly specified. If the affirmative recommends that a specific technology be made available, that technology must be identified and distinguished from other similar means. The plan plank may put forward a number of different options available to a group of decision makers who must choose among them. This permits the policy to have greater flexibility.

In general, the plan should be as concise as possible. A lengthy plan reduces the amount of time the affirmative has to develop its case.

QUESTIONS FOR DISCUSSION

1. In what speech is the affirmative usually presented?

2. A plan plank is _____.

ACTIVITIES

1. Having researched the harm, significance, and inherency in the previous activities, now outline a possible solution to the problem.

2. Using the plan outlined in the activity on page 77, try to anticipate possible solvency arguments and outline answers to them. Now research these answers.

3. What disadvantages (harms) might result if the affirmative plan outlined on page 77 were put into place? Make a list of the possible harms of the plan.

CASE FORMATS

A *case format* is a plan for arranging affirmative arguments in such a way that they can be clearly expressed and easily remembered. The case format suggestions made in this section are not meant to be ironclad rules. Case formats must be adapted to the skill levels of the debaters and to the requirements of the topic.

The Need-Plan Case

A *need-plan* case is comprised of a statement of the proposition, explanation of terms, a statement of problems impacting on the present system, suggestions as to the causes of the problems, a plan, and proof that the plan will eliminate the causes. The case might also include a statement of additional benefits to be brought about by the plan. The following outline is one way to construct a case.

Statement of the Resolution
Definition of Terms
Presentation of Affirmative Plan

Contention I.
(on need)

There are significant problems in the present system.
A. The problems exist.
B. The problems violate substantial values. (harm)
C. The problems are widespread and growing. (significance)

Contention II.
(on inherency)

The causes of the problems are inherent in the present system.
A. The status quo policy does not cover all or part of the problem.
B. Those policies designed to cover the problem do not work.
C. The structures of attitudes and incentives suggest that the problem is more likely to grow worse than to terminate on its own accord.

Contention III.
(on solvency)

The affirmative plan will solve the problem.
A. The affirmative plan fills in the gaps left by the present system.
B. The affirmative plan corrects the defects of present system policy.
C. When tried in another context, the affirmative plan worked.

The need-plan case is a standard format. Even if you wish to argue other kinds of cases, it is best to begin your work on a topic by framing such a case. It permits clear identification of the range of issues and strategic options involved in working with a topic.

1. What are the components of a need-plan case?

2. It is up to the affirmative to decide how many harms to include in the affirmative. How many should be used? Why?

ACTIVITIES

1. Using the arguments you outlined earlier, formulate them into a need-plan format.

2. Write an eight-minute first affirmative speech using the need-plan format.

The Comparative Advantage Case

The *comparative advantage case* is comprised of a statement of the resolution, presentation of the affirmative plan, and the support of one or more comparative advantages stemming from the plan. A comparative advantage is stated in the form of a contention that an effect stemming from the plan will have a positive impact on the present system. The case format may include an overview that suggests a general problem area in which conditions of improvement may be made. Consider the following outline:

Statement of a General Area of Policy Concern
 A. The problem has been with us for a long time.
 B. The problem area is a legitimate government concern.

Statement of the Resolution
Definition of Terms
Presentation of the Affirmative Plan

Advantage I.   The affirmative plan will bring about benefit X.
 A. Present policy does not have benefit X. (inherency)
 B. The plan is sufficiently efficacious to achieve benefit X. (solvency)
 C. Benefit X is significantly desirable. (significance)

Advantage II.   The affirmative plan will bring about benefit Y.
(alternative   A. Benefit Y is significantly desirable. (significance)
structure)   B. Present policy cannot obtain benefit Y. (inherency)
 C. The plan is likely to achieve benefit Y. (solvency)

Advantage III.   The affirmative plan will bring about benefit Z.
(alternative   A. Similar plans have brought about benefit Z. (solvency)
structure)   B. These plans have been eliminated or curtailed by the present system.
 C. Benefit Z is very desirable. (significance)

There are three considerations in preparing a comparative advantage case. First, the affirmative can argue for any number of advantages. The more time it spends on developing one, the less time it will have to develop others. Second, each advantage is a miniature case. The advantage must establish that an important benefit will accrue from the plan and that the benefit is not likely to be part of the present system. If the negative can prove that the advantage is not inherent, significant, or does not obtain the advantage, then the contention is lost. Third, the substructuring of each comparative advantage may vary. In the outline, the different advantages all contain the same concepts, but the order of the stock issues within the advantage results in slightly different case development. The affirmative should choose the structure and wording of contentions that best suit the purposes of persuasion.

The comparative advantage case is quite useful in developing independent lines of analysis that show it is better than the present system's policy. If a policy is cheaper, more efficient, and more comprehensive than that offered by the present system, there may be substantial reason to adopt it—even if the policy cannot eliminate an enduring or long-term problem. It may be that pollution, poverty, and crime will be part of United States society for a long time to come. If the affirmative can identify policies that create better solutions to these problems than those currently in practice, clearly such policies ought to be adopted.

Summary

The comparative advantage format is employed by many modern debaters. Its development is nearly as simple as the need-plan format. It offers a greater range of choice for issue development. The affirmative need not focus on a single harm, but can identify a whole range of benefits. In such debates, it is critical to refute the negative disadvantages because the whole point of the case design is to compare the respective merits of the present system policy and an alternative.

QUESTIONS FOR DISCUSSION

1. What are the elements of a comparative advantage case?

2. What are the three important considerations in preparing a comparative advantage case?

3. What is the difference between the comparative advantage case and the need-plan case? How would you determine which case format to use?

ACTIVITIES

1. Using the harm issues given earlier, (p. 74) outline a comparative advantage case.

2. Write an eight-minute first affirmative constructive speech using the comparative advantage case format. Present the speech.

Other Case Formats

There are a host of variations on the two basic designs. These formats include the criteria case, so named because the criteria for advantages are spelled out, and the goals case, so named because the objectives of the present system are explicitly compared to its efforts in a policy area. Such formats are beneficial to debaters familiar with basic case developments. However, at this point, it is better to become well acquainted with the use of basic case formats. Even the most sophisticated and complicated case structures developed by very experienced advocates are only variations on the basic outlines presented in this chapter.

EXTENDING AFFIRMATIVE ANALYSIS

Once the case is written and presented by the first affirmative, the negative has the opportunity to probe for weaknesses and to refute affirmative contentions by establishing that the harm is not significant, not inherent, or not capable of solution by the plan. To make sure that the affirmative case is defensible against such attacks, debaters should imagine potential negative attacks and create answers to possible objections. It may be difficult to imagine every possible negative argument, but with a little work the affirmative can become well prepared to extend the analysis presented in the case.

Is every contention supported with sufficient proof and reasoning? The most typical negative response to a claim is to probe the sufficiency of evidence supporting the contention or subcontention. To assure that you will not be caught short on any of these probes, use the following check list when developing your affirmative case.

Affirmative Checklist

1. Are the sources of opinion cited to substantiate the claim reliable?
   a. Are they experts in the field?
   b. Are they unbiased?
   c. Is their testimony recent?
   Are sources of opinion who disagree with your contentions reliable? What could lead them to hold erroneous opinions?

2. Is there substantial evidence to suggest that a large number of people are hurt by the failure of present system policies? If there is not substantial evidence on the numbers of people, are there any other reasons why it can be inferred that a large number of people are or will be hurt by the policies?

3. Are the harms really that significant? Is there evidence to suggest that people really do care or ought to care about the problem? Are there any situations with comparable harms in which policy action has been taken?

4. Is there a trend to suggest that present policies may be effective in eliminating the problem? Can current programs be given just a little more support and become effective in eliminating the problem?

5. Are there barriers to the affirmative solution of the problem? Are there barriers to achieving affirmative benefits? Are there other causes of the problem that might impede plan solvency?

These are the attacks that are likely to occur. The affirmative ought to be prepared to refer to the initial evidence established in the first affirmative constructive. If the questioning is extensive, additional evidence ought to be supplied for consideration.

What possible improvements could be made, short of the proposition, that would make the plan unnecessary? Once these arguments are established, refutation can be prepared. For example, against an affirmative that attempts to correct the fee-for-service medical care system with universal socialized medicine, a negative might say that the present system can be repaired by establishing small group practice organizations. This is more efficient than fee-for-service but less drastic a change than socialized medicine. The affirmative must be able to refute this argument, pointing out how the repair will not work or has been tried and failed. The affirmative must predict the minor repairs available to the negative and construct briefs that refute their efficacy.

What are the potential disadvantages of the plan? Of course, not all teams argue the same disadvantages against a case. And even if an affirmative encounters similar disadvantages, they are somewhat differently structured and argued in each round. Nevertheless, it is important that the affirmative develop briefs to dispatch alleged harms created by the plan. Since the affirmative cannot know in advance the extent to which a disadvantage will be developed, it is wise to prepare two kinds of arguments: one that includes a few good responses to the disadvantage (in case it is not important) and another that goes into great depth (in case it is). Especially when you are arguing for a comparative advantage case, it is very important to determine potential lines of disadvantage and to prepare counter-refutations.

ACTIVITY   1. Using one of your first affirmative speeches outline possible negative arguments.

STYLE AND THE AFFIRMATIVE POSITION

Putting together a workable affirmative case is a difficult and complicated task. The negative has the edge, it would seem, because the affirmative carries the burden of proof. If the affirmative makes a mistake, it might lose the debate even though only one or two arguments are wrong. Despite these problems, however, learning to debate the affirmative is very important.

In real life, many decisions are made on quite narrow grounds. To accept a change, people want to be reasonably certain that the change will improve conditions and not make them worse. By requiring yourself to make the best possible case for a resolution, you will be improving your own ability to make trustworthy appeals for policy changes that affect people's lives. Submitting your work to a strong challenge by the negative is difficult, but in the end it is worthwhile.

One of the keys to success in debating the affirmative is finding a cause you believe in. Most topics are broad enough to offer a variety of case areas for discussion. Find a problem that you find personally repugnant and see if there really is a way to correct it. The more real the problem seems to you, the more real you can make it appear to the audience. To be sure, there are *moving* situations in the world today—famine, terrorism, denial of human rights, ecological destruction—to name just a few. Debating these problems should involve much more than a dull exchange of information and statistics; it should involve language that communicates something of the true horror of the problems and that appeals to the consciences of people everywhere to move toward resolution. In debating the affirmative you are establishing a logically complete case, of course, but you are also doing more. An affirmative is a call to action. It says that there is something wrong in the world and that we can and must do something about it. However technical the arguments become in any debate, the affirmative must find the language necessary to describe the particular pathos of the harm, the frustration with policies rooted in political expediency, the joy of finding new solutions, and the satisfaction of a job well done. These are the emotions that must be infused into the evidence and reasoning in any case.

8

The Negative Position

Life is filled with change or compromise. In your future, you will be faced with situations where you feel a proposed change is not enough, not appropriate, not effective or unnecessary. When that happens, how will you convince others not to implement the suggested change? It is unlikely that you will be in a position to say "no, because I say no." Instead, you will need to justify your position. Learning to debate the negative will teach you to analyze and challenge positions, to look for alternatives to change and to identify the disadvantages of a particular change. It also helps to develop courage. To accomplish these tasks, you will need to understand the following key terms:

causal argument	negative strategy
causality	refutation
circumvention	sign argument
counterexample	testimony
counterplan	trend argument
counterposition	workability
minor repairs	uniqueness

The basic duty of the negative position is to defend the present system. There are many theories about constructing successful negative arguments and strategies against affirmative cases. Some of these will be covered in this chapter. Basically, the debater should remember that there are two fundamental positions against any affirmative case. First, the negative may choose to deny that the affirmative has established sufficient proof or evidence for its claim. Second, the negative may choose to deny that the claim itself is true. Consider each alternative.

DENIAL OF THE PROBLEM

Challenging Affirmative Proof

In Chapter 7 we learned that the burden of proof is on the person arguing for a change. Thus, the affirmative has to prove the truth of its contentions and with the affirmative plan provide a reason to adopt the proposition. The negative need not prove anything in a debate, if the negative team can demonstrate that the affirmative has failed to meet its burden of proof. Here is an example of this point: Suppose someone claims that he has seen a blue piece of paper. If he cannot present any evidence that he in fact saw a blue piece of paper, there is no reason to accept the claim. The negative would not have to prove that the piece of paper was not blue, but green or red or some other color. All the negative would have to do is to ask for some kind of proof. And, in the absence of proof, the claim could not be established. Even if the affirmative produced some evidence that the claim was true, if that evidence were tested and found to be questionable or unreliable, there would be no reason to accept the claim. Thus, the negative has the option to argue against the affirmative by questioning the existence of proof or its reliability.

Counterposition

The negative may wish to do more than challenge the reliability of the affirmative support. The negative might want to establish the real truth of the matter. To do so, the negative creates a *counterposition*. A counterposition says that the real truth is other than what the affirmative says it is. In the example of the blue paper, the negative may choose to prove that the paper is actually red. They would then be refuting the affirmative claim by inference: because the paper is red, it cannot be blue. If the negative chooses this type of refutation, then it assumes a burden of proof. The negative must show that there is enough evidence to accept the counterposition. If the burden of proof can be met, however, the negative has a powerful refutation of the affirmative claim. This type of refutation proves the claim is actually wrong.

Combining Types of Refutation

In most debates, the negative combines both types of refutation. If the strength of the affirmative proof can be weakened, and at the same time the believability of a counterposition can be established, then the negative is in an excellent position to win an argument.

Conceding the Argument

Sometimes the affirmative proof is simply too strong to overcome. An affirmative argument may be true! In such a case, the negative may choose not to refute the affirmative argument but to concede its truth. Concessions are not necessarily bad. A concession on one argument permits the negative to attack a more weakly supported contention. The negative should explain why the truth of the argument is not important when deciding if a change should be made. For instance, it may not be necessary to deny that there are homeless people in the United States. It may make more sense to prove that government housing can solve the problem.

Remember, then, when you begin to consider responses to an affirmative case, you have four possible positions on any given argument: (1) refute the adequacy of affirmative proof, (2) establish the truth of a counterposition, (3) combine challenging the proof and establishing a counterposition, or (4) concede the argument but explain why the truth of the argument is not important to deciding the desirability of the policy. No matter how complicated thinking about the negative position may become, these are the basic options.

Applying the Types of Refutation

Now that you understand the choices for refutation, consider how refutation may be applied to an affirmative case. Consider the situation of a general planning a battle. Like a general, your purpose is to defeat an opponent. In planning your operation, you need to think about conducting the attack on three different conceptual levels. You must decide how each soldier will fight another. A battle is composed of groups of people maneuvering about and leading attacks and counterattacks. The general must decide upon the tactics of engagement. A general also must have an overall battle plan that gets the soldiers to the right place at the right time and organizes the tactics in the best way to defeat an opponent. Consider how this analogy explains the levels of refutation in a debate.

At the level of individual argument, the negative must know how to attack the claims made by the affirmative. Rather than fighting with bows and arrows, or machine guns and hand grenades, the debater uses verbal argument. The negative refutes the affirmative claims by arguing that the evidence used is untrustworthy or that the reasoning from the evidence to the truth of a claim is unsound. There are many ways to indict evidence and reasoning. Some of the most important ones will be discussed in this chapter.

Summary

At the level of clusters of arguments, the negative must know how to attack a major stock issue. The affirmative chapter established the stock issues: harm, significance, inherency, solvency, and disadvantages. The negative must know how to argue that its combination of proof challenges. Counterclaims constitute a substantial reason to believe that the stock issues are on the negative side when the debate ends. Just as a general has to decide how to use his troops in combination for tactical victories, so the negative must be able to use combinations of arguments to defeat the affirmative stock issues.

At the most basic level the strength of all refutation must be taken into consideration. Before a battle, a general must decide where the enemy is weak and gather resources to attack that point. He must also decide where the enemy is strong and figure out how to avoid clashing at these points. Before a debate, the negative must decide at what point the affirmative arguments are the weakest and prepare evidence to attack this position. Thus, the negative must examine alternative combinations of attacks on stock issues and decide where and how to use its resources.

Though each level of analysis is different, all are important. A general could not win a battle if he had good soldiers, but poor tactics and strategy. He could not win if he had good soldiers and tactics, but poor strategy. He could not win if he had admirable tactics and strategy but poor soldiers. Similarly, a negative cannot win if there are good particular arguments but a poor use of these arguments and an inconsistent strategy, and so forth. It is important to think of the possibilities and burdens of refutation at each level of analysis.

QUESTIONS FOR DISCUSSION

1. What must the negative prove in the debate? Why?

2. When considering responses to any affirmative case, the negative has four possible positions on any given argument. What are they?

ACTIVITIES

1. If the negative can demonstrate that the affirmative has not met its burden of proof, the negative does not have to prove anything. Illustrate this with an example other than the one given in this chapter.

2. Using your example from Activity 1, create a counterposition.

3. Using the proposition and affirmative case outlined below, complete the following task:
   Is there a counterposition? If so, outline it. If not, explain why.

Resolved: That an environment conducive to teaching and learning should be provided in the elementary and secondary schools.
   I. The problem of school violence is widespread and growing.
      A. Many attacks on teachers and classmates have occurred. Students and teachers have a right to security.
      B. Present disciplinary procedures do not discourage violence.
         1. Psychological referral is inadequate.
         2. Security personnel are limited by expense.
         3. There is a lack of communication among parents, the schools, and the courts.
      C. Increased violence can lead to repressive social policies.
   II. Alternatives to present disciplinary procedures are desirable.
      A. Tougher suspension policies can increase discipline.
      B. Student participation can increase discipline.
      C. Television monitoring and more security can increase discipline.
      D. Revamping juvenile courts can isolate violent students.
      E. The present system has taken no steps to implement any of these solutions. It is unlikely that it will do so in the near future.
   III. The affirmative plans help to curtail school violence.

4. Using the affirmative case outlined above, identify the affirmative weak points.

REFUTATION OF INDIVIDUAL ARGUMENTS

There are many ways the affirmative can support a claim and many ways the negative can refute one. This section of the book will identify some of the most common methods of offering and refuting proof. It may be difficult to memorize all of the different ways to challenge evidence and reasoning. But effort directed at becoming familiar with the tests of support will be valuable. Each test you learn will increase your ability to refute arguments. The following tests of reasoning will include examples from policy debates in order to illustrate the importance of these arguments.

Refutation of Generalizations

A generalization simply says that a particular statement is true because a number of instances or examples support the statement. If an affirmative wishes to establish the claim that all United States military interventions are bad, one way to do this is to present examples of interventions and point out their harmful consequences. The list of interventions might be long. If the affirmative indicted nearly all interventions, the proof would appear conclusive. What opportunities does the negative have to refute this reasoning?

Time frame   One important way of testing the reasoning of a generalization is to ask whether the examples cited cover a reasonable period of time. Several mistakes are possible. First, the examples of harmful interventions may be dated. It is possible that interventions in the 19th or early part of the 20th centuries turned out badly, but that more recent examples turned out differently. The negative would want to show why there is a difference between examples from the distant past and those more relevant to the present—and future. Second, the examples of harmful interventions may have occurred during a short period of time when there were problems peculiar to that era. Perhaps the bad interventions occurred at a time when America was toying with the idea of imperialism. And, without an imperialistic motive, perhaps interventions over the long run reflect a wise policy. Third, one needs to consider the generalization as a truth extending into the future. Even if all past examples of interventions have proven unfortunate, this does not necessarily mean that future invasions of foreign nations will have the same results. If the negative can show there are different conditions that will produce successful interventions, then the affirmative examples are not relevant to the claim. When all past examples support the affirmative generalization, the negative must prove that the future will be different from the past.

Number of examples   Another test of a generalization is to see if a reasonable number of instances are cited to support the claim. If there are only a few examples and if the claim is quite broad, then the affirmative (in this instance) has committed the fallacy of hasty generalization. In establishing that interventions are bad, affirmatives often resort to Vietnam as an example in which a lot of American lives and money were wasted. It may be the case that Vietnam is not representative of the risks inherent to interventions. Even if one or two other examples of unsuccessful interventions could be provided, like the Bay of Pigs invasion in Cuba and the mining of harbors in Nicaragua, still—as measured against the backdrop of hundreds of successful United States interventions—it is not necessary to conclude that these "atypical" examples justify the generalized claim. A negative might strengthen this claim by showing why the few examples presented are unique or atypical and by showing why the generalized rule of successful intervention policy will pertain.

In many cases, the notion of what constitutes a sufficient number of examples is a matter of judgment. If an affirmative cites a few examples, the negative cannot just claim that it wants to see more. Rather, the negative must show that the examples given are insufficient. One reason might be that of simple proportion. If there are thousands of instances, a generalization from one or two does not seem sufficient. Another reason is that of risk. If the claim is important, then it is desirable to have a significant amount of confirming evidence. Also, if authorities say that intervention is on the whole a good policy, then the affirmative is obligated to present a more comprehensive analysis. Whatever the particular reason, the negative must establish why the proof in question is not proportional to the conclusion.

Counterexample   A counterexample throws the affirmative generalization into doubt. At a very minimum, the counterexample establishes that there are significant exceptions to the affirmative generalization. These exceptions must be taken into account when judging the reliability of the affirmative claim. If the generalization that all interventions are bad is challenged by the fact that the invasion of the Dominican Republic saved American lives and property, then one may be able to conclude that sometimes interventions are good and sometimes they are bad. In this instance, the negative would argue that intervention as a policy ought to be preserved. One should simply avoid the bad or dangerous interventions. Should there be a sufficient number of timely counterexamples the affirmative would have to abandon the claim.

Relevance   A basic test of reasoning to a generalization is to verify that the examples cited are actually instances of the rule asserted. If the generalization were put forward that interventions are not harmful, and the examples included, say, covert operations, economic aid to military regimes, and rescue missions taking place during Vietnam, then the number of harmful interventions might seem small in comparison to the number of successes. The negative might point out, however, that these other so-called interventions are not really examples of the generalization. They are actions much smaller than a full commitment of troops in the field. Looking at the number of "real" interventions might lead to a much different generalization. Thus, the negative should examine the examples to see if some can be declared irrelevant to the general rule. This tactic permits counterexamples to carry more comparative weight in testing the general rule.

QUESTIONS FOR DISCUSSION

1. A generalization says a particular rule is true because _____.

2. What are the tests of a generalization?

3. What role does time play when the negative is challenging affirmative generalization examples?

4. Define a hasty generalization.

5. When you are proving a generalization, how many examples are enough? When the number of examples is sufficient, how should the negative refute the generalization?

6. One way to refute a generalization is with counterexamples. How important is the quality of the example? What will be the impact of significant counterexamples?

ACTIVITIES

1. Outline two examples of a hasty generalization (using evidence). Outline (with evidence) a negative response.

2. Select a speech and identify any generalizations and how they would best be refuted. Why? For examples of speeches consult *Vital Speeches, Congressional Quarterly, Representative American Speeches, Time,* etc.

Refutation of Causal Argument

A *causal argument* is important to debate. An affirmative may wish to isolate the causes of a problem to prove that the present system's policy cannot solve the problem for one of two reasons: 1) it is not equipped to deal with the causes or 2) it is only equipped to deal with the wrong causes. Additionally, the affirmative always argues that the proposed policy will bring about effects that will solve a problem or at least create a condition that is better than the one created by the present system. The negative must be prepared to refute both types of causal claims.

Finding the real cause of a problem

Policy analysts sometimes confuse the "fundamental" cause of a problem and its intermediate causes. Consider a simple example. What causes poverty? At one level, the answer might be a lack of funds. When one is poor one is destitute. But what causes a lack of funds? One answer is that the poor do not have work. If this were true, then one could assume that work programs would solve the problem of poverty because they would provide people with money. The problem with this analysis is that it does not go far enough back and ask the question, What is the cause of joblessness among the poor? It may well be that the poor do not work because they do not have the skills and training. A cause of this problem may be that a culture of poverty influences the poor to give up. By not tracking the chain of causes and effects back far enough, the affirmative has failed to get at the root of the problem. Should the "real cause" persist, the affirmative plan may not be able to eliminate a set of undesirable social effects.

Multiple causality

Large social problems are usually not the result of a single cause, but the result of a number of interlocking causes producing an effect. In the case of poverty, its causes seem to be numerous. The "culture of poverty," for example, serves as a general term that includes numerous reasons why the poor remain in a state of hopelessness. The lack of a job, a decent home, education, medical care, protection against crime, and so forth may all contribute to a psychology that keeps people poor for generations. If an affirmative can discover a basic cause of a problem, then it may have a better chance of effecting a solution. However, the negative should, in addition to questioning whether authorities are in agreement that the single cause is valid, see if there are other major contributing causes to the problem.

Counteracting causality

Even if the affirmative is able to establish a relationship between policy in the present system and social problems, it still might run into problems when it compares the future of the present system under an affirmative plan to the future of the present system without the affirmative plan. There might be some other causal factor that also caused or significantly contributed to previous relationships. This new factor might interrupt the causes of the present system and possibly prevent the affirmative from achieving its solution to the problem.

Return to the poverty example for a minute. One of the causes of poverty is unemployment, which leads to such ill effects as spouse and child abuse, hunger, and lack of adequate medical care. If enough people are unemployed, however, wages might become cheaper and industry might be able to reemploy more workers and reverse the economic cycle. Thus, there is a counteracting cause that is a self-corrective mechanism within the present system that permits adjustment before the problem gets too bad. Note that even if the economy does not bounce back, there are mechanisms that stimulate hiring and limit the severity of unemployment. For example, fiscal and monetary policy act as counteracting causes to the problems of poverty. The negative should look for present system mechanisms designed to moderate social problems. These mechanisms can furnish grounds to claim that the affirmative harm is not inherent.

Another important area for counteracting causality arguments is the solvency of an affirmative plan. It may be the case that the affirmative plan takes certain steps that unintentionally trigger causes that hamper its ability to reach a solution. If the affirmative wished to solve the poverty problem by guaranteeing every United States citizen a cash income, then poverty would be solved because no person would be destitute. Everyone would have money. No one would be poor. Right? No. By giving the poor cash, the government would create a demand for more goods. Stores might simply raise their prices and those who could afford to pay would get the goods. The poor would have money, but they would not be able to buy necessities. Because the affirmative initiated a counteracting cause—increasing demand, which increased prices—and because the counteracting cause intervened between the plan and its desired effects, the affirmative would lose the solvency issue. The negative should look for side effects of the affirmative plan that work as causal factors that militate against the solution of the problem.

QUESTIONS FOR DISCUSSION

1. Define the two types of causal arguments.

2. Outline three ways the negative can challenge the causal argument.

3. Counteracting causality can be used to refute the affirmative _____, as well as the affirmative case.

ACTIVITIES

1. Using each of the claims below, identify (with evidence) alternative causes.
   a. Poor farm management is the cause of many farm foreclosures.
   b. Water supplies are being destroyed by chemical waste dumping.
   c. Spending for social programs has been cut to finance increases in military spending.
   d. Student test scores are declining because of teacher incompetency.
   e. Poverty is responsible for the malnourishment of America's poor children.
   f. Welfare programs encourage the unemployed poor to remain jobless.

2. Each of the social problems listed below has multiple causes. Identify them.
   a. Poverty
   b. Air pollution
   c. The federal deficit
   d. Energy shortages (past and future)
   e. Agricultural farm foreclosures

Refutation of Sign Arguments

A *sign argument* says simply that when x appears so does y. It does not say that x causes y or that y causes x. It says that the two are related much like symptoms and a disease. For example, any time you have the sniffles you know you have a cold. If you have been exposed to people with colds, you know that you are likely to get the sniffles. Sniffles are characteristic of a cold. The cold is the substantial term given to a particular type of disease. A sign argument can either take known characteristics and reason to a conclusion, or it can take a conclusion and reason to the kind of characteristics that are to be expected.

Sign arguments are useful to the affirmative when the cause of the problem is unknown, but it is necessary to know the nature of a problem so that its symptoms can be treated. If there was an outbreak of a certain kind of disease, one might conclude that it is related to certain substances that ought to be under the control of an inspection system. It may be the case that a certain dairy has become contaminated. The spread of disease does not show why the system has failed, but it does locate the nature of the failure in inspection and suggests a direction for treatment.

Sign arguments are useful especially when you are considering a problem that is just emerging but has yet to be fully identified. If one or two undesirable cases are identified, then—given the nature of the cases—one can be assured that an undesirable state will emerge. In recent arms control negotiations with the Soviets, the president has argued that any reduction in military spending will send a sign to the Soviet Union of America's weakness and that continuing such signs will embolden the Soviet Union to be even more militaristic in the future. Here the signs point the way toward a future problem.

Do the signs point in a single direction? It may be the case that there is more than one set of signals (or signs) relevant to judging the likelihood of an existent or future harm. In the arms control negotiations, a vote on the MX missile might be read as a signal of weakness to the Soviet Union. However, given that the United States Congress has allocated trillions of dollars to defense spending and is rapidly building a huge arsenal of modern weapons, it cannot be said that the signs are consistent. The negative should try to assemble countersigns that indicate that the problem is not emerging or at least that there is substantial doubt at this point in time about the existence of the problem.

Where does the affirmative place its emphasis when telling (or proving) the argument? If a situation includes both signs and countersigns, you must distinguish minor or incidental signs from important signs that can lead to an informed judgment about the nature of the substance. For example, the MX debate could be a sign of the weakness of the American will, or it could be a sign of prudence on the part of Congresspersons who do not want to waste money on weapons that are unnecessary or will not work. Put in the context of the thousands of weapons systems presently being built, a vote against the MX cannot be interpreted as a telling sign of American will. Of course, if the argument could be made that this was the most powerful and essential weapon of the time, then a vote against the MX could be a *telling* sign, perhaps a beginning point for the country's eventual capitulation. Lacking any other such signs of surrender, however, it is difficult to make such an argument.

A *telling* sign is one that establishes an intrinsic relationship between the characteristics and the substance. An intrinsic relationship is one in which the character always accompanies the substance. When the sun is behind the earth, it is night wherever you are. Because knowledge of an intrinsic relationship is usually not available, conflicting signs must be interpreted by preponderance of evidence. Where do most of the signs point? Are the signs that point in a given direction the most important ones—that is, are they the signs that almost always accompany the substance? To win a sign argument, the negative must do more than uncover the presence of conflicting signs. It must show that, to the contrary, these signs are more important than those isolated by the affirmative.

QUESTIONS FOR DISCUSSION

1. When are sign arguments most useful to the negative?

2. What are the two tests of sign arguments?

ACTIVITIES

1. Using the resolution and case below, develop negative arguments using sign argument.

Resolved: That the federal government should establish a comprehensive program to significantly increase the energy independence of the United States.

   I. U.S. energy dependence is harmful.
      A. U.S. is dependent on foreign oil imports.
      B. This dependence causes inflation.
         1. Inflation causes unemployment.
         2. Inflation causes death and suffering.
         3. Inflation reduces economic output.
      C. The present system cannot solve the problem because energy independence is not a goal of the present system.
  II. Fossil fuels will run out.
      A. Fossil fuels are finite.
      B. There is a need to develop alternative energy sources.
      C. The present system cannot develop alternative sources because it lacks a comprehensive national energy program.
 III. Affirmative Plan
      A. A five-member energy board with all necessary powers will be created. All necessary staff and facilities will be provided. All members will be required to retire at age seventy, with a replacement to be appointed by the board.
      B. Duties of the board:
         1. Oversee programs for solar energy.
         2. License buildings equipped for solar energy.
         3. Oversee research and development of alternative energy sources.
         4. Provide tax incentives for conservation.
         5. Provide tax incentives for insulation.
      C. Funding will be by a mix of cutting tax loopholes, elimination of duplicative programs, and cutting defense spending.
      D. Enforcement by fines and/or imprisonment.
 IV. Advantage: Solar energy is the best energy alternative.
      A. Solar energy is cheap.
      B. Solar energy is effective.
      C. Solar energy is renewable.
      D. Solar energy is technologically feasible.

Refutation of Testimony

Testimony is a statement of opinion. An opinion is necessary to provide proof where empirical evidence is not available, either because no study has yet been done to specify the harm or cause of the harm in question or because no study is possible. When no study is possible, opinion functions to provide authoritative evidence as to what *ought* to be society's goals and values. Such evidence can come only from opinion because questions of purpose can be resolved only through cooperative discussion. In testing the affirmative case, the negative needs to be concerned with any testimony that is cited. Here are the major tests for this kind of evidence.

Is the testimony from a respected source?

One of the present aspects of publishing is the proliferation of a number of sources of information that are without credentials. These include newspapers sponsored by members of the ideological extremes, left and right, and scandal sheets that are sold in grocery stores all over the country. Often, such unreliable information is quoted in academic debate without even a blush. Such evidence is used because it makes unequivocal claims that no responsible person or institution would make. There are no homeless in America. There is no hunger in America. Cancer is cured. Aliens have invaded from outer space! If any of these claims were true or even likely to be true, then a debate might be quite different, but their truth is so suspect that no other source even bothers to comment on their falsehood. To determine whether such "testimony" is part of the affirmative's case, the negative should examine the affirmative's sources. If an affirmative uses a number of sources without credentials, this should become a major issue in the debate.

Does the testimony reflect a consensus of expert opinion?

Testimony that has been confirmed by a majority of experts knowledgeable in a field is compelling proof. If climatologists, using a variety of models, all agree that the world's weather is getting warmer, then there is a consensus from which reliable policy can be formulated. On the other hand, if it can be shown that there is substantial disagreement among experts, then even if some reputable people are convinced as to the correctness of their own conclusions, the formulation of policy may be premature. The obligation of the negative in this case is to point out simply that disagreement among experts requires that the judge vote on the basis of presumption. Without compelling proof, there is no reason to change the present system.

Is the testimony disinterested?

If the person providing the testimony has something to gain by the acceptance of a policy, then his or her motives can be questioned. Consider, for example, a debate on the use of nuclear power. If the affirmative's testimony showing that nuclear power is cheap, safe, and reliable comes from representatives of utility companies, it is legitimate to ask whether the testimony can be trusted, without support from more neutral experts. On the other hand, the negative must guard against this charge, particularly in defending the present system. It may be that some representatives of government agencies are more interested in defending the administration's policies than in acting in the public interest. Recent leaders of the Environmental Protection Agency often testified that problems of pollution were overstated and that their agency was making progress with deliberate speed toward enforcing pollution standards. However, several congressional investigations and firings showed that even high government officials cannot always be trusted.

Is the testimony recent?

When it comes to contemporary problems, recent opinions are prized. The reason is obvious. If an authority is describing a situation that existed ten years ago, the evidence may no longer be relevant. To say that the United States economy is "in a mess," as President Reagan did when he took office, was true during the early recession of the 1980s. But the recession has passed and with it the value of the testimony. Especially where situations are rapidly changing, it is important to use contemporary opinion. The more recent, the better.

The negative should remember, however, that recency is not an absolute value. In most cases, it really doesn't matter that the date of one opinion is a day or even a month later than the date of another opinion. What is crucial is to explain why more recent testimony is more trustworthy—to show that changes have occurred that might render past judgments unreliable. Yet, again, in some instances sources that have withstood the test of time may be more valuable than an up-to-the-minute report. Surely, if one were discussing the fundamental values of American society, it would be better to quote Adams, Jefferson, and Washington than the latest issue of *Newsweek, Time,* and the local gazette. Opinions of well-trusted sources on enduring questions are more trustworthy than this week's journalistic essay, which becomes tomorrow's trash.

Are the values of the source and the community consistent? Some sources who are regarded as experts in a special field may maintain views inconsistent with the overall precepts of democracy. Marx is an expert on communism; Krapotkin, on anarchy; and Louis XIV, on monarchy. But debate does not operate in a world in which values are determined by allegiances to communism, anarchism, or monarchism. Each of these ideologies devalues argumentation and debate as processes of decision making. Debate can only deal with opinions that exist within the framework of democratic values.

Sometimes the test of value agreement is more subtle but no less important than in the instances just examined. Suppose an authoritative source is quoted to the effect that freedom is the most important democratic value. Nothing less than the Declaration of Independence and the United States Constitution can be cited here. Suppose further that a right-wing gun control lobbyist is quoted as saying that hand-gun control is a significant violation of freedom. Has a substantial argument been made? Not necessarily. The value of freedom may enjoy widespread support from experts and the public alike. The particular violation in question, however, may not be very significant. The lobbyist's claim may reflect more of a concern for keeping his or her own gun than a commitment to democratic values. The negative should make sure that the reasoning process that links together statements about values employs respectable sources throughout the argument.

QUESTIONS FOR DISCUSSION

1. Testimony is defined as a statement of opinion. What are the strengths and weaknesses of testimony as evidence?

2. What are the five ways to challenge testimony?

ACTIVITIES

1. The following examples of testimony are flawed. Identify the problem with each.

Resolved: That the federal government should establish a comprehensive long-term agricultural policy in the United States.

a. "Homeless in America," *Newsweek,* January 2, 1984, p. 2.

"Because they live without addresses, the homeless are unable to receive food stamps and welfare in most states, invisible in unemployment statistics and impossible to count. Estimates range anywhere from 250,000 to 2 million nationwide, tens of thousands of whom hazard the elements every night."

b. The World Bank, "Drought in Africa," *The Economist,* September 10, 1973, p. 45.

"Africa is the only part of the world which now grows less food for each of its people than it did 20 years ago. In nine countries food production per head is less than 90% of what it was in 1950. Nearly 200 million people—more than 60% of Africa's total population—eat fewer calories each day than the UN thinks are required to provide a survival diet."

c. *The New York Times,* December 18, 1985, p. A8.

"There are no longer any emergency conditions in the 20 countries affected by the drought. The goal to feed the hungry in these countries appears to be accomplished."

d. Shona McKay (writer, *MacLeans*), "How Drought Engulfed a Continent," *MacLeans,* November 7, 1983, p. 59.

"Said Oxfam's Gallagher: 'This system provides people with a subsistence living when conditions are normal. Under drought conditions, it means they face starvation'."

e. John Glenn (senator), *Famine in Africa,* Committee on Foreign Relations, U.S. Senate, January 17, 1985, p. 7.

"I've seen one estimate that indicates that the Sahel region in Africa is expanding southward at about 8 miles per year. This climatological condition is unlikely to be altered until the world goes through its 11- or 22-year cycle of weather changes."

2. As you did in the previous activity, identify the problem in each of the following examples of testimony.

Resolved: That the federal government should establish a comprehensive national policy to protect the quality of water in the United States.

a. J.E. Tiernan (Resources for the Future), "A Rational Evaluation of Cancer Mortality Associations with Treated Drinking Water," *Journal of Environmental Health,* November-December 1983, p. 124.

"More epidemiological studies on drinking water and cancer mortality are essential. Our natural resources are rapidly being depleted and the effects of the degradation of our water must be soundly proven before it is too late."

b. William Ruckelshaus (EPA Director), *Groundwater Protection: The Quest for a National Policy,* 55th Report by the Committee on Government Operations, October 4, 1984, p. 9.

"If we discover gaps in terms of our ability to protect ground water, either with our own responsibilities or those of the States, we will investigate ways to fill those gaps. If, in order to implement our responsibilities and the States' responsibilities, we need to develop a national ground water policy, then I will do that."

c. Tom Kelley, "Enforcement Drive Mounts," *EPA Journal,* November 1978, p. 7.

"In the fiscal year since then, 28 corporations and individuals have been convicted in federal courts of environmental crimes, a dramatic increase from 11 in FY 1975, nine in FY 1976 and 11 in FY 1977. Twenty-four other cases, including fifteen involving illegal dumping of waste, have been referred to the Justice Department for prosecution and some 160 cases are currently under investigation."

d. James J. Floyd (president, White's Chemical Research Group), "Reliance on Disposal Does Not Present a Future Problem," *The Environmental Forum,* October 1985, p. 20.

"The current disposal rate of chemicals into landfills and nearby streams does not pose an immediate danger. Those chemicals being dumped are harmless and the cost to clean up the landfills and streams to their original state would be minimal."

REFUTATION OF STOCK ISSUES

The discussion of the kinds of refutation available for particular affirmative claims should have suggested to you how stock issues may be refuted. This section looks at strategies for refuting such issues in greater detail. Each stock issue is supported by a number of affirmative claims that require individual attention.

Harm or Advantage Each affirmative case indicts the present system. The indictment can be of two kinds. First, the affirmative can say that the present system is doing something wrong. This is called a harm. Second, the affirmative can say the present system is *not* doing something it ought to do or could be doing. This is called an advantage. A case that focuses on harm tries to get rid of a bad policy. A case that focuses on advantage attempts to establish a beneficial policy. Both concepts are similar insofar as the affirmative tries in both to identify a change in policy that will leave the world better off, rather than worse.

Often, it is difficult to show that a problem identified by the affirmative is not harmful per se. The age-old scourges of famine, poverty, disease, war, and economic instability are too well accepted by the community to be discarded as not harmful. Rather, the affirmative claim as to the "significance" of the harm or the advantage is what is usually contested.

Seriousness of the Harm The negative can mitigate the significance of a harm by showing that the harm is not as serious as the affirmative contends. For instance, most people agree that going without a job is a social harm. There are a number of present system laws that state that the objective of a just society is to provide work for all citizens. If the negative can demonstrate, however, that much unemployment is voluntary, then the harm may not warrant action. Also, if people choose to quit their jobs in order to look for better work, they may be suffering a harm but fulfilling another value, the right of free choice and voluntary association. By putting the "harm" in the context of a necessary evil to fulfill a higher value, the negative undercuts the affirmative rationale for change.

Necessity of the Solution Occasionally, the affirmative harm or advantage is based on the present system's failure to meet optimal policy goals. The advantage of a new policy, the affirmative argues, is its ability to meet a problem more comprehensively, faster, or less expensively. Here, the negative needs to be able to separate essential from incidental values. For example, although it might be desirable to have a car with many extras, they may not be worth the increased costs.

By analogy, it might be argued that even though increased funding to education would result in better programs, current funding is sufficient to cover the essentials of a basic education. By distinguishing core or central values from peripherals, the negative can reduce the increment of affirmative advantage or mitigate the perception that the status quo is inadequate.

Requesting Quantification

Another way to reduce the harm or significance is to request quantification of a problem or an advantage. If the affirmative case says that farm policy should be changed because present policy is driving farms into bankruptcy, then the negative can legitimately ask about the number of farms being foreclosed. If the affirmative cannot provide overall quantification, then it cannot be assumed—in spite of several spectacular instances of farm failures—that there is a national harm. Moreover, the negative has a right to ask about the impact of the alleged harm. Even if farm foreclosures are high, it may be the case that the farmers do not lose everything because they are protected by bankruptcy laws. Even if the harm is widespread, if its impact in individual cases is not great, there may not be a substantial reason for change.

QUESTIONS FOR DISCUSSION

1. What are the two ways the affirmative can indict the present system?

2. How can the negative mitigate the significance of the affirmative harm?

3. What is the difference between essential and incidential values? Provide an example.

4. If the affirmative can prove that a harm exists (or that the case gains an advantage), must it also prove that the harm or advantage is significant? Why?

ACTIVITIES

1. Using the following affirmative case, outline negative arguments with evidence to refute the affirmative advantage.

   I. Affirmative Plan:
      A. Phase out federal government crop loans, price supports, and commodity purchases or, in the alternative, phase out commodity purchases and limit crop loan prices and target prices to a figure set below prevailing world market prices. Convert the USDA to an agricultural research and farmer education focus.
      B. Plan administration through the Office of Management and Budget, in conjunction with the USDA. Government officials in violation of the plan mandates will be removed from office, fined, and imprisoned, private parties to receive fines three times the amount of government funds illegally obtained and to be imprisoned.
      C. Plan funding will be through general federal revenues or from sale of government-held commodities as needed.
   II. Advantages:
      A. Increased competitiveness of US agriculture.
         1. U.S. aids to agriculture increase the price of U.S. agricultural products: target prices, crop loans subsidize farmer production at costs above world market prices.
         2. U.S. agriculture is export-dependent: production levels assume competitiveness: option A, no government supports for farmers; option B, supports are limited by world market prices.

     B. Avoid inefficient government subsidies.
       1. Most government agricultural aid goes to farmers in stable financial condition.
       2. Farmers in financial trouble are not saved by commodity programs (PIK) or price supports: their problems are from production glut, low prices, which price supports aggravate.
  III. Inherency Arguments:
     A. Incrementalism: government perceives solution in adjustment or modification of current programs.
     B. Political perceptions: providing money to farmers creates a political illusion of assistance. Political motives guarantee continuation of aid.
     C. Support programs are incapable of solving the problem: by guaranteeing that the government will purchase crops, they encourage increased production.

2. Using the energy affirmative case on page 95, outline negative arguments with evidence to refute the affirmative harm.

3. Present a 3-minute speech, using your arguments from either Activity 1 or Activity 2.

Inherency   Inherency establishes that the causes of a problem exist within the practices and policies of the present system. The negative position on inherency is to deny that the causes of the problem have been isolated or that the present system can adjust and eliminate the problem. There are several methods that can be employed to deny the inherency of a problem. (Note that a team arguing a comparative advantage position still has the burden of inherency. The advantages must be shown to be unique to the affirmative plan. If the negative can demonstrate that the present system is in the process of achieving the advantages, then it proves there is no rationale for the affirmative plan.)

Trend arguments   One way to show that a problem is not inherent is to demonstrate that the present system is moving as rapidly as possible toward the end desired by the affirmative. This helps put the problem into perspective. If the affirmative argues that there are a significant number of people without access to medical care, for example, the negative can respond that over the past twenty years a combination of increased insurance coverage, health maintenance organizations, and government programs have made health care available to 95 percent of the population. In terms of the overall population, 5 percent may seem like a lot of people, but when put in the perspective of expanding coverage, the problem does not seem to be serious. Furthermore, if the negative can isolate the factors that will assure the expansion of the present system into the future, then the problem can with some confidence be ignored. Such a trend argument requires the negative to show that the problem has been reduced and will continue to be reduced.

Minor repairs   A *minor repairs* argument states that while there is some defect in the present system, the required remedy does not call for a substantial change in policy. If medical care has been denied to some people simply because of a lack of administrative coordination between various health service organizations, then the negative could advocate a procedural change. Rather than enacting, say, socialized medicine to solve the problem of health care access, all that is needed—the negative says—is a minor repair to a health care system that works well otherwise. If the minor repair is less costly and less risky than the affirmative plan, then the negative wins the debate.

To argue a minor repair requires that the negative assume certain burdens of proof. First, the negative must show that the minor repair does not intrude on affirmative ground. Especially when arguing broad, vaguely constructed resolutions, the negative must be careful that the repair cannot be subsumed as part of the proposition. The negative must be able to show that the minor repair can be made within the present system without adopting the affirmative proposition. Second, the negative must prove that the repair will work. Because the negative is making the claim that the real cause of the problem is other than that claimed by the affirmative, the negative must show that the repair is sufficient to remedy the situation. Third, the negative must be prepared to demonstrate that the minor repair has no undesirable side effects. Just as the affirmative must refute disadvantages to its proposed plan, so the negative must refute harms that might come about if the minor repair is made.

Discretionary powers   A commonly made negative argument is that individuals make choices (have discretion) about their decisions. It would be wrong to conclude, for example, that all the nation's environmental laws are inadequate just because of the administrator of the Environmental Protection Agency. That he or she is corrupt, incompetent, or both is no reason to conclude that the system as a whole is bankrupt. The negative position is that, given an adequate test, the present system can be expected to do a good job. The problem rests with the discretionary powers the administrator has and not with the structure of the present system. All that needs to be done is to enforce the law or to fund the program at reasonable levels.

The strength of this position is that it appeals to fairness. Yet, it can be taken too far. Some teams argue that because Congress can adopt the affirmative plan the problem cannot be inherent. This is an invalid argument because the issue is what should be done, not who should do it. That Congress can adopt an affirmative proposal does not indict the fact that at present the legal and administrative systems are such that the problem goes without solution. So, too, it might be reasoned that the failure to use discretionary powers is a sign that the problems of the present system are perpetuated only by attitudes, predispositions, or interests that prevent solutions.

However, if the affirmative can demonstrate a consistent pattern of neglect, the argument that the present system possesses discretionary powers is meaningless. On the other hand, if there are good reasons for maintaining discretion and if there is not a consistent pattern of abuse of discretion, then the negative may have a viable position.

QUESTIONS FOR   1. The negative denies inherency by denying _____.
DISCUSSION
2. Describe three ways the negative can argue against inherency.

3. What burden of proof does the negative assume when running a minor repair?

4. What makes the discretionary powers argument strong?

ACTIVITIES

1. Using the two cases on pages 95 and 100, outline arguments against each case's inherency. Try to use each of the three techniques described in this chapter, but not necessarily in each case.

2. Using the arguments outlined above, write a three-minute speech and deliver it.

3. Obtain an actual affirmative case (perhaps one prepared by someone in your class for the activity on page 83). Prepare a first negative constructive speech attacking the case (using the methods discussed earlier). This speech should be approximately four minutes in length and should include evidence.

4. Select a bill currently being debated in Congress (or one that was debated, if it pertains to the proposition you are debating). Study the arguments being used by the negative speakers against the bill. What type of negative arguments are they using? What issues are being raised?

Solvency (Efficacy)

Solvency challenges the affirmative plan's ability to solve the problem isolated by the proposition. In a need-plan case, solvency questions the ability of the affirmative plan to solve the problem by eliminating its causes. In a comparative advantage case, solvency questions the ability of the affirmative plan to bring about its stated benefits or advantages. Solvency arguments can be either directed against the specific affirmative claims made in the case or brought up as new considerations. In either case, the negative asks for rejection of the affirmative case on the grounds that it simply will not solve the problems the affirmative claims that it will.

Workability

A *workability* argument questions whether the plan can work. Even if the affirmative has isolated the correct causes of a problem, the plan must be capable of doing something about them. A plan that proposes to assure adequate medical care for all American citizens by establishing a national program with adequate funding and good intentions might run into severe problems if there are not enough doctors, nurses, or hospitals available to provide care. Furthermore, even if the affirmative assures money for training and facilities, there may be a limit to the number of talented, dedicated people who wish to go into this area. Workability issues focus the debate on the availability of resources, technology, or manpower. If there is a significant shortage of any of these components, the plan will not work.

A good affirmative case will attempt to establish proof for its workability by showing that the policy worked in the past, that a similar policy has been implemented elsewhere with good results, or that a pilot project seems likely to succeed. Even though there are substantial theoretical problems with wage and price controls, for instance, they did work well during the last World War. Even though there are objections to water pollution control laws on the grounds that unregulated pollutants inevitably seep into the waterways, a program of pollution control in the German industrial Ruhr valley was successful. Even though there are reasons to suspect the usefulness of "safe homes" for abused wives, pilot programs in Austin, Texas, and Madison, Wisconsin, have worked well. In each of these instances, the workability of a contemporary national program is suggested by a policy analogy.

Confronted with such evidence, the negative has several possible options. First, if the analogy is drawn between the proposed policy and one that is no longer in effect, then the negative might be able to prove that the analogy is inappropriate because conditions have changed. For example, although wage and price controls were acceptable during World War II, such controls might not be supported today by the general public. If public support is crucial, then the plan may not work.

Second, if the analogy is drawn between the proposed policy and one in effect in another country, then the negative might translate the differences between nations into different policy effects. The German industrial system might be different from our own in significant ways. However, the fact that Germany is a European country and the United States is part of America does not invalidate the analogy. If pollution control laws work similarly in industrial democracies, then the comparison may be legitimate.

Third, if the analogy is between a pilot program and a national program, then some attention might be given to the unique qualities of a small program. It may be the case that the local program has taken only the most easily solved cases or that its work can be conducted only within a limited range of communities.

Circumvention   A *circumvention* argument says that the problem will continue in the present system because ultimately the attitudes that allow the harm to exist will not be changed. This argument is common among advocates of the private ownership of guns. "Guns don't kill. People do." This slogan reflects the argument position that if handguns are banned people will find other ways to commit crimes against one another. Because the policy treats the symptoms of a disease as its cause, the problem is likely to continue in a different form.

A good affirmative case will attempt to create a system of incentives to prevent circumvention. By combining rewards and punishments, a policy can create a framework that maximizes the chances for successful cooperation. One of the major problems with toxic chemicals, for example, has been industrial dumping. In some cases, tank trucks simply drive down the road and open the valves. This happens because the treatment of toxic wastes is costly. Rather than comply with government regulations, companies take illegal action. A proposed solution has been to provide free toxic waste treatment and money for good waste cleanup procedures. This would eliminate the incentive to pollute. The negative must not take such a solution at face value. If greed and willingness to engage in criminal behavior are at the root of the problem, then it should be asked how these motives can reappear under the affirmative plan. In this instance, the polluters might take the money and produce even more toxic waste under the assumption that the government will clean it up. If this happened, increased costs might make the plan infeasible.

QUESTIONS FOR   1. Define solvency as it applies to a need-plan case and a comparative
DISCUSSION   advantage case.

2. What is the difference between a workability argument and a circumvention argument?

3. In what ways will an affirmative try to prove the workability of its plan?

4. When an example of a past program or an analogy to a similar program that was successful is used to prove workability, what approach should the negative take?

5. How do incentives in the affirmative plan help the affirmative get around circumvention arguments? How can the negative counter this tactic?

ACTIVITIES

1. Using the cases presented on pages 95 and 100, outline possible solvency arguments. These should include both workability and circumvention arguments. When possible, use evidence. When evidence is not available, develop the argument with reason. Be sure to show how the argument applies to the affirmative plan.

2. Using the arguments outlined in Activity 1, write a three-minute speech and deliver it in class.

Disadvantages

A *disadvantage* is a harm caused by the affirmative plan. In a sense, a disadvantage is the most important stock issue for the negative. Even if the affirmative harm is not as significant as the affirmative claims and even if some portion of the harm can be solved by the present system and even if the plan does not solve a part of the problem, as long as a small part of the harm can be solved by the affirmative, there is a reason to vote for the proposition. It is possible for the negative to win many particular arguments and still lose the debate.

A disadvantage works best in combination with other negative arguments. The negative attack on the case is designed to reduce the amount of harm that needs to be and can be solved by the plan (or the advantages delivered). Questioning the solvency of the plan, too, serves to reduce the affirmative rationale for change. Disadvantages are the negative side effects of the affirmative case.

There are several steps in constructing a disadvantage. It is best to think of the burden of proof for establishing a disadvantage as comparable to the affirmative's obligation in building a case. Disadvantages must be constructed with the same care and logical precision required of the affirmative case. The major difference, of course, is that a disadvantage ultimately proves why the plan creates a unique, compelling harm sufficient to reject the affirmative. The most powerful disadvantage would conclude that, even if all the affirmative arguments are true, the case should not be adopted because its side effects are so terrible.

The harms of the affirmative plan

These harms are of two types. The first includes harms that result because the affirmative plan would increase the problem rather than solve it. If the affirmative claims to solve poverty but produces a plan so expensive that it leaves people poorer than they were before, the proposition is undesirable. If the adoption of a particular type of weapons system is so costly and ineffective that it makes the United States more—not less—vulnerable to attack, then the case is without merit. In these instances, the disadvantage claims that the solution adopted by the affirmative plan increases the harm isolated by the case. This is an effective type of disadvantage because it offers a straightforward comparison of means to achieve a common value.

The second category includes harms different from those isolated by the affirmative case. An affirmative might claim to stop the drug problem in the United States by increasing border inspections. To do this could damage good relationships with some allies. An affirmative might claim to provide more jobs for people, but the program might create such undesirable side effects as pollution and inflation. In these instances, the harm of the disadvantage is not the same as the harm in the present system isolated by the affirmative. In such cases, the negative must show that its harm is more significant than that of the affirmative.

In cases where the affirmative advantage and the negative disadvantage are based on different values, the negative has the responsibility to establish the comparative merits of its argument. Sometimes this is easy to do. If the affirmative advantage is only one of greater efficiency and if the disadvantage involves the loss of human life, it is easy to argue that life-threatening concerns are more important. More often, however, the value judgments are quite difficult. Suppose an affirmative plan raises American standards of living at the expense of using up nonrenewable resources from impoverished nations. Which one should receive priority? The answer is unclear. Nevertheless, the negative must be prepared to construct a value position that explains why its harm ought to be considered more important than that isolated by the affirmative.

The relationship between the plan and the harm

The negative must isolate the reasons the plan will bring about the harm (the link between plan and disadvantage). If a plan uses up limited resources, the relationship between plan and harm is obvious. Resources used for one program cannot be used for another. If a plan creates an obvious violation of human rights or constitutional privileges, again the link is obvious. Most links between plan and harm, however, depend on a controversial claim to the effect that a bad situation is made worse by the affirmative plan. For instance, assume that trade relations between the United States and its allies, such as Japan, are deteriorating. While an import quota for a single commodity, like sugar or beef, will usually not cause a trade war, under present circumstances even a single-product quota may be the final increment of causality necessary to cause a trade war. This argument resembles the story of "the straw that broke the camel's back." Each straw does not weigh much, but there is a limit to what the camel can carry. Similarly, to the extent that the negative can demonstrate that the present system is close to this threshold of harm and to the extent that the plan can be shown to exacerbate problems in the direction of the harm, a disadvantage can be argued. The argument simply asks the judge not to accept the affirmative plan because of the risk that it will end in disaster.

The relationship of the disadvantage to the present system

If the present system creates the same disadvantage as the affirmative plan, then the disadvantage cannot be a reason for rejecting the affirmative plan. Because the disadvantage is not unique to (caused only by) the affirmative plan, it does not constitute a reason for rejecting a proposition. Consider the following scenario for a disadvantage linked to massive expenditures by an affirmative plan. The negative may argue that such expenditures will result in fragmenting the budget-cutting consensus necessary for sound deficit reduction programs and that a growing deficit threatens economic stability. If the affirmative can show that other budget-busting programs are in the process of passage, then the consensus is doomed to be fragmented whether the affirmative plan is approved or not. Deficit spending is no reason to reject the affirmative plan. The negative must provide reasons why the present system is not susceptible to the same type of "disadvantage" as the affirmative plan is.

Summary The negative can attack several stock issues offered by the affirmative. It can question the existence or significance of harm and advantage, challenge the inherency of the problem or the uniqueness of the advantage, refute the solvency of the plan, and demonstrate substantial comparative disadvantages.

QUESTIONS FOR DISCUSSION

1. A disadvantage is a _____ caused by the affirmative plan.

2. Is it possible for the affirmative to win only part of its inherency and part of its harm and have only partial solvency and still win the debate?

3. Why are disadvantages important to the negative position as a whole?

4. What are the steps in constructing a negative disadvantage?

5. The harms resulting from the affirmative plan can be of two types. The first argues that the affirmative plan makes the harms it isolates worse instead of better. What is the second type of harm?

6. Why must a disadvantage be unique to the affirmative plan?

ACTIVITIES

1. Using the affirmative cases on pages 95 and 100, outline possible disadvantages. These disadvantages should be proven with evidence.

2. Using the arguments from Activity 1, prepare a four-minute speech establishing the disadvantages that will result if the affirmative plan is adopted.

3. Select a bill currently being debated in (or recently adopted by) Congress. What are the possible disadvantages of the bill? Outline.

4. Using the debate proposition to be used in class debates, prepare a series of generic disadvantages that could be used against many specific affirmative cases under the proposition. Be prepared to justify your choice.

THE NEGATIVE STRATEGY

The negative has many options in a given debate. Considering just the stock issues previously discussed, the negative can argue any one particular stock issue or a combination. The choice of negative attacks is called a strategy. A strategy exhibits a plan of action to defeat the affirmative position. Strategies vary widely.

One strategy is to argue any and everything that comes to mind, with the hope that some arguments will go unrefuted by the affirmative. This "shot-gun" approach is overrated for two reasons. First, the arguments may contradict each other. How can a judge make sense out of the claims that the present system will solve the problem with no effort and that a considered plan of action can do nothing about the problem? How can consistency be derived from a position that repairs the present system to solve a problem and at the same time says that any efforts toward solution will result in immediate, massive disadvantages? Contradictions reduce the credibility of the negative position. Second, rattling through a number of arguments reduces the time and effort necessary to develop a detailed, complete, memorable argument. Some of the negative arguments are quite complex and must be developed as carefully as an affirmative case.

At the opposite end of the spectrum is a strategy that concentrates on only one stock issue. This, too, is a difficult strategy to sustain, if for no other reason than that it creates a very strong burden of proof for the negative and permits the affirmative to win most of its arguments without contest. Good strategy requires that a number of arguments be placed together in combination. This section will discuss some alternative strategic choices.

Topicality

In a beginning analysis, topicality need not be emphasized because most beginners follow the guidelines of the topic without clever deviations. Yet, because topicality is a strategic option for negative argument, it must be discussed.

The first thing to note is that topicality ought to be used in few instances because it is really a preemptive issue. If topicality is not established, then none of the arguments in the round really matter. To say that the affirmative is not topical is equivalent to saying that the case presented is not relevant to discussion. If this is true, then topicality ought to be argued exclusively. This makes for either a short debate or a long one that turns mostly on word tricks. On the other hand, topicality is a legitimate consideration and can be argued if the affirmative has somehow violated the expectations of the debate community.

Let's look at an example. If the proposition for debate is "Resolved: that school campuses should be open" the affirmative will probably be challenged on topicality if it argues for keeping the buildings unlocked on Saturdays and Sundays. Why would this affirmative not be topical? The negative would argue that the terms of the proposition refer to students being allowed to leave campus when not in scheduled classes. This is known as an "open campus." An affirmative case to open the building when students are not present is not relevant to the discussion, and therefore lacks topicality.

Because topicality is a preemptive issue, it ought to be argued by itself. When it is unclear that the affirmative has lived up to the expectations of the proposition or has exceeded them altogether, topicality can be used in combination with other arguments.

QUESTIONS FOR DISCUSSION

1. What does it mean to have a negative strategy? Is there one set negative strategy?

2. One negative strategy is the "shot-gun" approach. Why is it overrated?

3. When does the negative argue topicality?

4. It is often said that if an affirmative case is not topical the negative need not make any other argument than topicality (that is, topicality is argued in isolation). Why?

Defense of the Present System

This is the most commonly argued negative position. There are many variations on the position. In its fullest development, the negative argues (1) that the harms to the present system are not as great as the harms brought about by the affirmative plan *and* (2) that the amount of harm potentially reduced by the present system is equal to, if not greater than, the amount of harm potentially reduced by the affirmative plan. One could defend the present system simply by comparing levels of harm or by comparing levels of solvency.

The negative may wish to defend the present system when the affirmative harm levels are overstated or when the present system has recently passed a program designed to eliminate the harms. In the first case, the negative needs to concentrate on proving that the affirmative testimony is invalid. Occasionally, this will be the case. In recent times, for example, there has grown up a whole literature on the benefits of health foods. Despite the vast number of books written by health food advocates, however, there may be little hard evidence to support their conclusions. In the second case, the negative needs to concentrate on proving that the new present system programs are not subject to the defects of the old programs. For example, since the topic committee formulated the farm policy proposition, Congress has passed a new and improved farm program. Thus, the evidence from 1985 predicting catastrophe may not be relevant to a new policy enacted in 1986.

Oddly enough, another way to defend the present system is to concede that nothing can be done about a problem. The negative would argue that taking action to solve the problem would only cause disadvantages. In some rare instances, it may be better to do nothing than to do something about a problem. For instance, the negative position might argue for greater study of the problem in order to avoid the disadvantages that would result from acting too soon.

QUESTIONS FOR DISCUSSION

1. What does it mean for the negative to defend the present system?

2. When would the negative want to defend the present system?

3. What is an alternative to defending the present system?

The Counterplan

The *counterplan* is a strategy that admits that the present system should be changed, but argues that the negative team's proposal is better than the affirmative's. It is the most complex strategy available to the negative. It is used frequently in advanced debate. Because of its complexity, beginning debaters should probably master the traditional negative strategies before trying a counterplan.

GLOSSARY

academic debate A debate that is approximately one hour in length. There are two teams and each team has two members. (See *debate*.)

advantages Benefits that will result from adopting the resolution.

affirmative The side which argues that a change should be made in the present system.

affirmative case The area of the proposition the affirmative wishes to discuss. This area is developed by the affirmative throughout the debate. The structure of the case includes justification for change, a plan, and the advantages of the plan.

alphabetical filing system An organized system that involves categorizing index cards into subject areas and arranging the subjects alphabetically.

American Statistics Index A monthly abstract and index publication with annual cumulations. It covers all statistical publications of the U.S. government, including congressional publications with substantial statistical data.

analysis Separating ideas and arguments into smaller units for individual study.

argument A process of reasoning from the known to the unknown—from evidence to a conclusion.

assertion An unsupported statement; a conclusion that lacks evidence for support.

audience debate A debate before a group of people who have no specific background in debate. A limited problem area is usually chosen because it is of more interest to the specific audience and will likely have a greater impact.

ballot The form the judge uses to record the decision of a debate round, the ratings or rankings of the speakers and teams and the judge's comments.

brainstorming The process of searching one's own mind for ideas that might be relevant to the proposition. This can be done on an individual basis or in a group. Usually the larger the number of people involved the larger the number of ideas that will be generated.

brief An outline of arguments and evidence supporting one side of a proposition.

burden of proof The affirmative's obligation to provide sufficient reason for adopting the proposition. If the affirmative does not present a significant justification for change, it does not fulfill its burden of proof.

card catalog A complete list of book titles in a library arranged by author, title, and/or subject.

card file An organized collection of evidence recorded on index cards.

case format A type of affirmative case structure. Examples include need-plan and comparative advantage.

causal argument Isolation of the cause(s) of a problem to prove that the present system cannot resolve the issue.

causal link The logical connection between two events or arguments.

causality The relationship between two things in which one is believed to cause the other.

circumvention To get around or avoid; says that the policy will have no effect, despite its good intentions, because its intent will not be obeyed.

clash Direct opposition to an argument.

comparative advantage case A type of affirmative case structure comprised of a statement of the resolution, presentation of the affirmative plan, and the support of one or more advantages (benefits) stemming from the plan.

Congressional Information Service Index An annotated listing of all government publications from the legislative branch since 1970.

Congressional Quarterly A weekly resumé of activities in Congress.

Congressional Record Government document that lists the daily activities of the House of Representatives and the Senate. Includes debate over bills of legislation as well as testimony asked to be entered into the *Record*. Printed daily.

constructive A constructive argument is one offered in support of or in opposition to, the resolution.

constructive speech Speech that ranges from eight to ten minutes in length and presents the major points made by each team.

contention A claim made by the affirmative or the negative. A single, declarative statement.

contradictory arguments Two or more arguments that cannot be true at the same time.

counteracting causality When comparing the future of the present system to the future with a particular policy there may be some other causal factor that will contradict previous relationships. This factor could interfere with a solution to a problem.

counterclaim A claim in direct opposition to the claim made by the opposition.

counterexample Establishes that there are exceptions to the generalization.

counterplan A negative approach which admits that the present system should be changed, but argues that the negative team's proposal is better than the affirmative's. Traditionally, the counterplan is given in the first negative constructive speech; and it is demonstrated to be nontopical, competitive with the affirmative plan, superior to it in the area of analysis attacked by the affirmative, and also less disadvantageous than the affirmative plan.

counterposition Contends that the real truth is other than that which the opposition claims.

cross-examination debate format A plan of organization where debaters are permitted to ask direct questions of an opponent during specified time periods, usually immediately following the opponent's constructive speeches.

debate A regulated discussion of a proposition by two matched sides. It provides reasoned arguments for and against a given proposition.

definition of terms Explanation of key words in the resolution so that the nature of the action advocated is clear to everyone concerned.

disadvantage A claim that the proposal will result in making harmful conditions worse or in some way create new harms.

discretionary powers Authority given to those in charge to make decisions and changes necessary to ensure the implementation and operation of the proposal.

eight-minute rule A rule that applies to the affirmative and the negative as a team. Each team is given a total of eight minutes' preparation time to use as it wishes. Preparation time is calculated from the time one speaker sits down until the next speaker begins speaking.

evidence Information used to form the basis of an argument; statements by someone respected by others, to support the argument the debater is making; such statements are usually found in newsletters, newspapers, magazines, news releases, journals, books, and interviews.

evidence card A four-by-six-inch or three-by-five-inch index card on which one records evidence. Only one piece of evidence is recorded on a card. Each card should contain a complete citation of the source used.

fiat The affirmative right to state that the machinery and personnel will be made available for the plan to come into existence.

first affirmative constructive speech Usually all inclusive. It includes contentions, case, plan, and advantages. All of the affirmative reasons for change are set out at the beginning of the debate.

first affirmative rebuttal speech This four- or five-minute speech is the affirmative's response to twelve or fifteen minutes of uninterrupted negative argument. The first affirmative rebuttalist must answer all new material presented by the second negative constructive speaker and extend case arguments which were refuted by the first negative rebuttalist.

first negative constructive speech The direct response to the first affirmative constructive speech. The negative may challenge the affirmative's definition of terms and topicality. Defends the present system by showing how it can solve the problems outlined by the affirmative.

first negative rebuttal speech Refutes, extends and develops the case arguments that were introduced by the second affirmative constructive speaker. This speech is half the time of the first negative constructive.

five-minute rule Same as the eight-minute rule but with a five minute limit. (See *eight-minute rule*.)

flow sheeting Process of taking notes during a debate. The goal is to follow the flow of the debate and accurately record all of the principle arguments of the debaters involved in the debate.

generalization A conclusion which states that a particular rule is true because a number of instances or examples support the rule.

harm A problem caused by the presence or absence of government policy.

implementation The method of putting a plan or program into effect.

index (guide) An alphabetical listing by author, title, and/or general subject of magazine articles that have appeared in a particular group of periodicals.

Index to Legal Periodicals A book, available at most university libraries, that lists all law journals. It is divided into three sections: 1) subject and author index; 2) a table of cases alphabetically listed by plaintiff's name; and 3) a book review section.

inherency Isolating the cause of the problem. If the cause is found to be a part of the current policy, then it is said to be inherent.

judge A person or a panel of three people who evaluate a debate against certain ideal standards of debating and decide who wins and who loses. Criteria includes analysis, reasoning, evidence, organization, refutation, and delivery.

justification Why the resolution rather than any other program should be adopted to correct the affirmative harms or gain the affirmative advantages.

key terms Words about or relating to the subject to be researched.

Lincoln-Douglas debate format   Involves only two participants (one on each side). A value proposition is used. The aim is to be persuasive before an audience with an emphasis on analysis as opposed to evidence.

logical reasoning   The process of explaining why a particular argument makes sense. Sometimes an argument can be explained to the satisfaction of everyone in a debate through common sense or with facts that are assumed to be true by most people.

minor repairs   An argument that the negative states. While there is some defect in the present system that will prevent the solution of the problem isolated by the affirmative, the required remedy is of such a minor nature that it does not warrant a substantial change in policy.

Monthly Catalog   An index to federal government publications.

multiple causality   A problem that may have more than one cause. This is particularly true of large social problems.

need-plan case   A format comprised of a statement of the proposition, explanation of terms, a plan, a statement of problems impacting on the present system, suggestions as to the causes of the problems, and proof that the plan will eliminate the causes.

negative   The side that defends the present system. Argues that although the present system might have a few minor problems, they are problems that can be solved without a major change (a new law, regulation, or rule).

negative block   The second negative constructive speech followed by the first negative rebuttal. This is twelve to fifteen minutes of uninterrupted negative speeches.

negative strategy   The choice of negative attacks. A plan of action to defeat the affirmative position.

notebook index system   A system of organizing index cards (divider cards) by number rather than by subject. A master notebook is then kept for the entire filing system. All of the material in each file box is noted on a single index sheet to which one can quickly refer for a code number that applies to specific subjects. Each major heading would receive a letter and each subcategory a number. The index sheet provides the summary for the filed material. Each card is numbered according to the index.

one-minute (two-minute) rule   A rule that applies to the individual speaker. Each speaker is allowed one (or two) minute(s) to prepare a single speech.

operational definition   Practice of defining the resolution through the presentation of the affirmative plan early in the first affirmative constructive speech. Individual terms are not defined, but rather the affirmative plan constitutes the essence of the resolution.

plan   Mechanism used by the affirmative to enact the proposition. It must provide for a complete method of enacting the proposition. It must specify who will enforce the plan, what action must be taken, what provisions must be made to assure adequate funding and access to resources and circumstances that might prove sufficient for exemption to normal operation.

plan-meet-need   A requirement that the affirmative plan be capable of gaining the affirmative needs or advantages.

preparation time   The time used between speeches for preparation.

present system   The current state of affairs; the laws, regulations, and rules that people live by.

presumption   The assumption that the policy now in effect should remain in effect. The feeling is that the values which led to the current policy will continue to exist and that what is currently accepted as true will continue to be accepted as true. Thus the affirmative side which always argues for change, is obligated to prove that change is necessary. Presumption usually favors the negative.

prima facie   A French term meaning "on face value" or "at first sight." The affirmative in debate must present a case that is complete "at first sight."

prima-facie case   A case that stems directly from the proposition and gives good and sufficient reason for adopting the proposition; the minimal argument required to support the proposition without refutation. Unless the affirmative team establishes a prima-facie case, it cannot win a debate.

problem area   A general question of some concern to a community or group of people.

proof   Evidence introduced to support the claim. Logical reasoning, evidence, or a combination of the two.

proposition   A statement that is open to interpretation. It is a statement about which reasonable people may accept arguments on either side.

proposition of fact   An objective statement that something exists. It asserts that a condition exists that can be verified by someone other than the person making the statement. A proposition of fact may be about some object or event that can be experienced directly by the physical senses of sight, hearing, touch, smell and taste. It is considered to be the simplest and least controversial of the three types of propositions.

proposition of policy A statement of a course of action to be considered for adoption. If adopted it is intended to guide present and future government and/or private sector decisions.

proposition of value A statement of judgment about the qualities of a person, place, thing, idea, or event; concerns opinions and attitudes; concerns a thing's qualities, rather than the thing itself.

reasoning Explains why the evidence supports the specific claim in question.

rebuttal speech A short speech devoted to 1) rebuilding arguments that have been attacked; 2) refuting opposing arguments; and 3) summarizing the debate from the perspective of the speaker.

refutation The process of attacking and destroying opposing arguments.

resolution A proposition that is offered for consideration. A resolution requires explanation, discussion, and proof. A proposition for debate should present a clear and important choice.

second affirmative constructive speech A speech with three primary purposes: 1) to re-establish the affirmative position in the debate; 2) to refute the major arguments presented by the first negative speaker; and 3) to extend affirmative arguments and present any remaining constructive materials for the affirmative.

second affirmative rebuttal speech The last speech of the debate. The aim is to put the debate in perspective and to continue to advance the affirmative's basic strategies in the debate. Explains what the arguments mean in terms of the context of the debate round.

second negative constructive speech A speech that deals with the affirmative plan. The primary purpose is to deal with the issues: 1) plan workability; 2) plan solvency; and 3) plan disadvantages.

second negative rebuttal speech Identifies the case arguments the negative views as voting issues and demonstrates that the significance of the disadvantages outweighs the advantages or the solvency of the affirmative harm.

shift To abandon an original position and argue for a different one.

should-would arguments Arguments based on whether the plan will be accepted rather than whether or not it should be accepted.

sign argument When one thing occurs so does another. Often we wish to use sign reasoning to get from known characteristics of a person, place, or event to an understanding of a phenomena. The sign identifies the characteristics. The signified is the object characterized.

significance The importance or scope of an issue.

solvency The ability of the plan to solve a problem or bring about an advantage.

"spread" Giving multiple responses (arguments) to arguments raised by the opposition.

standard debate format A debate format using ten-minute constructive speeches and five-minute rebuttal speeches with no questioning periods.

stock issues The basis of major affirmative contentions. Stock issues include: harm, significance, inherency, solvency, side benefits, and disadvantages.

ten-minute rule Same as the eight-minute rule but with a ten minute limit. (See *eight-minute rule.*)

testimony Statement of opinion. Testimony is acceptable evidence in debate if it is from a qualified expert.

timekeeper The individual who keeps track of each debater's speaking time and lets the speaker know how much speaking or preparation time has elapsed. The timekeeper does this with time cards. The time is counted down in minute increments until the last minute, when 30-second increments are used.

topicality A strategic option for a negative argument. The state of conformity to the intent of the debate resolution. A case is topical if it justifies the full intent of the resolution.

trend argument A demonstration that the present system is moving as rapidly as possible toward the end desired.

uniqueness Affirmative advantages must be unique and must result from the implementation of the affirmative plan. The negative disadvantages must also be unique and must result from the implementation of the affirmative plan; the plan must be the causal factor.

Vertical File Index A listing of materials from pressure groups, foundations, academic departments, think tanks, and other organizations. The index is carried by most libraries and the library will order materials for it on request. It also lists organizations from which pamphlets may be ordered directly.

workability The ability of the plan to solve the problem outlined.

The page references in boldface type indicate key terms.

NOTES

NOTES

NTC DEBATE AND SPEECH BOOKS

Debate
Advanced Debate, *ed. Thomas and Hart*
Basic Debate, *Fryar, Thomas, and Goodnight*
Cross-Examination in Debate, *Copeland*
Getting Started in Debate, *Goodnight*
Judging Academic Debate, *Ulrich*
Modern Debate Case Techniques, *Terry, et al.*
Strategic Debate, *Wood and Goodnight*
Student Congress & Lincoln-Douglas Debate, *Fryar and Thomas*

Forensics
Coaching and Directing Forensics, *Klopf*
Creative Speaking, *Buys, et al.*
Creative Speaking Series:
 Extemporaneous Speaking, *Buys*
 Group Reading: Readers Theatre, *Beck*
 Humorous Dramatic Interpretation, *Cobin*
 Oral Interpretation, *Hunsinger*
 Oratory, *Scott*
 Radio Speaking, *Beck*
 Serious Dramatic Interpretation, *Cobin*
 Special Occasion Speeches, Miller
Forensic Tournaments: Planning and Administration, *Goodnight and Zarefsky*
Forensics as Communication, *ed. McBath*

Speech Communication
Contemporary Speech, *HopKins and Whitaker*
Creative Speaking, *Buys, et al.*
Getting Started in Public Speaking, *Prentice and Payne*
Listening by Doing, *Galvin*
Literature Alive!, *Gamble and Gamble*
Person to Person, *Galvin and Book*
Person to Person Workbook, *Galvin and Book*
Self-Awareness, *Ratliffe and Herman*
Speaking by Doing, *Buys, Sills and Beck*

Resource Materials
A Guide for Teaching Speech Today, *ed. Halliday*
Creative Drama in The Classroom Grades 1-3, *Cottrell*
Creative Drama in The Classroom Grades 4-6, *Cottrell*
New Horizons for Teacher Education in Speech Communication, *eds. Newcombe and Allen*
Noncompetitive Speech Activities, *Buys, Copeland, and Eisenhardt*
Speech Communication, *Galvin and Book*
Speech in the Jr. High School, *Herman and Ratliffe*
Teaching With Creative Dramatics, *Cottrell*

For further information or a current catalog, write:
National Textbook Company
4255 West Touhy Avenue
Lincolnwood, Illinois 60646-1975 U.S.A.